To Mend, to Make

How NLP helps me in my roles as a Writer, Mentor, and Storyteller

Judith Woodrow

Edited by
Ms Peanut Woodrow

This edition published by Notion Press

This edition published 2024

To my grandma

Thank you for always being my inspiration,
Ammachi.

Mend, Make or Bend, Break

Articulated perceptions may help or harm
Declared resolutions may humiliate or charm
Verbalized assumptions hurt or heal
Enounced thoughts make a humble man of zeal

Sea of Language is a gift to Mankind
Sky of words is food for a sane mind
A garden of phrases entices human souls
Word stocks cultivate the wisdom of life goals

Tower of Dreams is built on mutual terms
The power of words frees everyone's mental squirms
Picking the right ones is the best of all arts
Think; Speak mindfully to conquer known hearts

Acknowledgements

When I began my journey into motivational lecturing, storytelling, and life coaching, little did I know that the principles of Neuro-Linguistic Programming (NLP) would profoundly shape not just my career but my life itself. This book is a reflection of how NLP became a bridge between my passion for connecting with people and my dream of inspiring meaningful change.

I owe my deepest gratitude to the brilliant minds behind NLP, Richard Bandler and John Grinder, whose pioneering work laid the foundation for this transformative discipline. I also extend my heartfelt thanks to linguistic thinkers like Noam Chomsky, Steven Pinker, Barbara Landau, David Crystal, and many others whose insights into the science of language and human behaviour inspired me to explore and refine my own storytelling and coaching techniques.

Books have always been my mentors, and I draw tremendous inspiration from works like *The Magic of Believing*, *Storyworthy*, *The Theory and Practice of NLP Coaching*, *Endangered Minds*, *Thinking, Fast and Slow*, *The Language Instinct*, *Behave*, and *Listen*. Each one has pushed me to delve deeper and strive harder in my writing and coaching journey.

This book would not have come to life without the incredible support of institutions and communities that believed in my vision. My gratitude extends to my teachers, professors, friends, family, and students. I thank the colleges, universities, schools, Parents and Teachers Welfare Associations, hospitals, the Coast Guard Wives Welfare Association, the Writer's Circle, and the Reader's Club. They were the stepping stones that encouraged me to take that very first step as a writer.

I owe special thanks to my daughters, who, in their own way, became my toughest critics and my greatest motivators. One day, my 8-year-old asked me, "Can I read your book?" I smiled and replied, "You might not understand everything in it." Her response was a simple yet profound challenge: "Then why don't you write it in a way kids like me can understand?"
Her question hit me hard, and it was then that I realised the power of simplicity. To simplify something for all age groups

means you must truly understand it yourself. My 14-year-old daughters, on the other hand, doubted whether I could rise to the challenge of keeping the writing clear and relatable. This became the first test of my application of Meta-modelling, a cornerstone of NLP, even before I wrote the first chapter.

What I've learned through this process is that simplicity is not about dumbing things down. It's about clarity, confidence, and connecting with the essence of what you want to convey. This book is a testament to that journey—a journey where I strived to reach minds and hearts of all ages and backgrounds.

To everyone who has supported me, believed in me, and inspired me along the way, this book is for you. Thank you for helping me turn this dream into reality.

Words are the invisible threads that weave human connections.

PREFACE

I'm happy to introduce myself as a Language Person. Although the roles I play using language as a tool may seem pretty distinct, each complements the others and makes my journey through life beautifully rewarding.

When I finally learned to balance the roles by managing my time wisely, integrating and combining them clearly, making my family understand and helping me manage the workload, my passion for these roles grew broader and deeper, and I became flexible and adaptable as time moved on.

My life was already transforming during my pregnancy with my second child then. As I prepared for this new chapter of motherhood, I came across Neuro-Linguistic Programming (NLP) Practitioner courses online. At first glance, I was reminded of my college days when I came across these concepts.

How could they be applied to everyday life? I had absolutely no idea this would be the foundation for both my personal and professional growth. We realised we'd implemented many of the NLP principles with our first daughter without knowing of them. Each stage of her growth aligned seamlessly with specific NLP principles. It was as though we had instinctively followed a roadmap, not knowing the names of the streets we'd passed. Relating to and naming those principles was like uncovering a hidden treasure in a way. We were thrilled and felt a deep sense of pride and validation in our parenting journey.

The results were promising as our second child grew up in a nurturing environment where we'd casually followed a few of these principles. We didn't make it hard, like following a crazy rigid rulebook, but we kept creating mindful and engaging moments. Without naming any of the procedures, we got used to them as a routine. Parenting became more of a joyful exploration of possibilities than we thought it to be. We wondered if NLP could make such a difference in our family and what it could do in other areas of life.

So, our journey to integrate NLP into my professional world began. At the time, I was leading a team of content writers.

Though every writer was unique and had their own writing style, I had to play an extra role as a mentor to teach them communication and writing skills. That's when NLP helped me a great deal. The results my attempts brought to the table were satisfactory.

Applying NLP concepts was kind of developmental in terms of time and space. One of the concepts of NLP is Anchoring. It's about creating connections that trigger the desirable responses. As a copyeditor and a content team manager, in the team meetings, I used to share my experience as a writer, interesting anecdotes, metaphors and short stories related to the daily day situations to motivate the team. Most of the team meetings began with a brainstorming session with a story, poem or an example from real life, and it became a team activity to share an interesting story first. Before, the team meetings were like mere formalities, but not after this practice. Ideas flowed naturally, and discussions became more dynamic and lively. The writers were so involved that they grew as a team. It was a rewarding experience for all of them.

I began my role as a mental health mentor as soon as I took up my role as a copyeditor. NLP came in handy in that role as well.

From helping clients reframe their thoughts to anchoring positive emotions, I was happy that I was able to help my clients empower themselves to take control of their lives quickly. Witnessing positive changes and rewarding transformations was hugely satisfying.

Around this time, I also began exploring storytelling as a medium. I have been an orator and a storyteller since school, but I used my storytelling skills only to participate in literary competitions and events. It was after my first daughter that I started using storytelling as an everyday activity.

Stories connect us with our audience effortlessly. They evoke emotions and inspire people to make positive changes in their lives. I was sure that combining storytelling with NLP would be very effective. And yes, it helped me craft narratives for my clients, mentor writers, and share my life experiences. Storytelling sure did help me reach my audience and make an impact.

On the other hand, my strong suit had been copywriting and copyediting since my college days, as I began my career as a copywriter in the content creation field. In the course of time, I learned to be precise and to focus on clarity every time I delivered content. Copywriting, evidently, complemented my Life Coaching and Storytelling journey. To me, a well-edited piece of writing is not just about good grammar, correct spelling, and correct punctuation, but it's about the ability to define ideas in a refined way to reach the target audience. Copyediting, as an extension to my life coaching journey, helps me guide my clients in communicating better than before.

What started as a simple interest during my pregnancy evolved into a multifaceted journey that intertwined my roles as a mother, a professional, and a lifelong learner. NLP changed my way of seeing the world and understanding people's perspectives.

This book is an invitation to join me on this journey. Along the way, I've gathered a blend of personal anecdotes, helpful insights, and some good ol' lessons. Whether you're a parent looking for ways to connect with your child, a professional seeking to enhance your skills, someone who would like to resolve issues with your partner in a relationship, or simply someone curious about personal growth, there's something here for you.

Life coaching, copyediting, and storytelling may seem like quite different paths, but for me, they're interconnected. They're all about understanding—understanding yourself, understanding others, and understanding the power of words. I hope that as you read this book, you'll find ideas that resonate with you, tools you can use, and inspiration to embark on your own journey of growth.

The beauty of this journey is that it's not about perfection; it's about progress. It's about discovering what works for you and using that to create a life that feels authentic and fulfilling. Whether you're anchoring positive habits, refining your storytelling, or learning to listen more deeply, every step counts.

So, let's begin this adventure together. Let's explore the principles, the stories, and the lessons that have shaped my journey and, hopefully, will inspire yours. Here's to growth, connection, and the endless possibilities that lie ahead.

Contents

A speaker's power is not in their voice but in the hope they ignite.

Where it All Started

As a life coach, storyteller, and copyeditor, I've always believed in the power of language. Language isn't just a way to communicate; it's a tool to connect with others and inspire transformation. When I first learned about NLP (Neuro-Linguistic Programming), it felt like a revelation. I realized how much it could help me personally and professionally. Naturally, I started experimenting with NLP techniques at home—my family became my first audience.

It all began when my younger daughter was three years old. She loved listening to stories, a habit that started practically at birth. One day, I decided to try something different. I read her a moral story about a boy who lies about a tiger. I made it engaging, reading it every day for a week. By the end of that week, she began repeating the lesson: "Lying is bad. Always speak the truth." She shared this wisdom with her sister and father in her adorable toddler voice, making everyone grin and melt. That moment showed me the potential of storytelling--- as a powerful NLP tool, too.

This storytelling tradition grew over time. We started creating our own stories, blending fun, creativity, and moral lessons. My younger daughter absorbed them eagerly, and this practice became a cornerstone of her growth. Today, she's eight years old, a budding writer, storyteller, and illustrator. She even visits schools and colleges as a young storyteller. Her language skills amazed us early on—her vocabulary was far ahead of her peers, and she had a remarkable ability to express her feelings and ideas clearly.

A Journey Into Writing

When she turned six, something extraordinary happened: she published her first book.

It started with her scribbling stories in a notebook, using her pencil to craft her ideas. Most of her spelling was correct, but what truly charmed us were the creative ways she made up her own rules. She decided that some words needed silent "e"s and that "k" sounded better than "c" in certain places.

When we asked her if she wanted others to read her stories, her response was a resounding "Yes!". That's when we started teaching her standard spelling rules and explaining why they were needed for readers to understand her work. She eagerly sought help from her elder sister for editing and even credited her as the editor at the end of the book. It was a proud moment for our family.

Her sister also illustrated the book, showcasing her artistic skills. The two of them worked together beautifully, sharing the creative process plus the royalties from book sales. Their collaboration definitely brought out the spirit of teamwork and showed how well they could do together.

Discovering Her Sister's Talent

You might be wondering how her elder sister, five years older, knew how to edit and illustrate. Here's an interesting backstory. From the time she was two years and one month old—just 25 months—we noticed her artistic abilities. One day, while scribbling in a notebook with a sketchpen, she called out, "Mommy, Daddy, come and see my happy caterpillar!"

To our amazement, her "scribbles" turned out to be a convincing drawing of a smiling caterpillar. Later that same day, she drew rough sketches of ducks and chickens walking, dancing, and even doing gymnastics. That's when we realized she was a born cartoonist. From then on, we made sure to nurture her talent. We bought her drawing supplies and encouraged her creativity. Over time, her skills improved, along with her love for stories. Although we weren't consciously using NLP techniques, many of the principles we followed—like engaging her in creative and mindful ways—mirrored NLP strategies.

Parenting with Balance

As parents, we've always strived for balance. We didn't want to push our children to become prodigies or burden them with unrealistic expectations. Instead, we focused on helping them enjoy their childhood while growing up with a sense of responsibility. Even during my pregnancy, I would read and sing aloud, creating a nurturing environment for the baby. After they were born, I used board books, flashcards, and nature walks to engage them. We spent quality time together as a family, playing educational games, telling stories, and having meaningful conversations.

Mealtime was another opportunity for connection. We would have dinner together most evenings, talking about dishes, ingredients, and recipes in a playful way. This not only made meals enjoyable but also helped our children connect with the world around them. By the age of two, my younger daughter could recognise the names of most vegetables. She enjoyed nearly everything we cooked and loved food-themed stories. If a story featured a vegetable or dish she knew, her excitement was infectious.

The Reading Milestone

To our surprise, she started reading at the age of three. She received a Dora the Explorer story collection of board books as a birthday gift, and we caught her slowly sounding out the small words. It was delightful to watch her pronounce "the" as "ta-heh" and figure out each word at her own pace. Instead of correcting her immediately, we let her explore and enjoy the process. Our use of phonics cards and playful teaching methods worked wonders, building her confidence and love for language. Our elder daughter, too, had a unique reading journey. She began reading slightly earlier, but the techniques we used were similar for both children. By the time our second daughter was three and a half, she had caught up and developed an impressive reading ability. Her passion for books quickly turned into a family habit, and our bookshelves began overflowing. We started visiting book fairs regularly, exploring new titles together, and turning these outings into cherished family traditions.

Relaxed Parenting and 360-Degree Absorption

What truly stands out in our parenting journey is the relaxed approach we took. We didn't impose strict schedules or high expectations. Instead, we created an environment where our children felt free to explore, learn, and grow naturally. This stress-free upbringing allowed their brains to absorb knowledge in all directions—what I like to call **360-degree knowledge absorption**. They didn't just learn from us or their books; they learned from their surroundings, conversations, and daily experiences.

This holistic learning process saw to that they grew up with a well-rounded understanding of the world, all while enjoying their childhood to the fullest. Whether it was identifying vegetables, creating art, or crafting stories, every activity became a learning opportunity without feeling like an ordinary chore.

Applying NLP Principles in Parenting

Looking back, I see how closely our parenting aligned with NLP principles, even though we weren't consciously applying them.

Multi-sensory learning played a key role as we engaged our children's visual, auditory, and kinesthetic senses through activities like phonics cards, storytelling, drawing, and cooking. By associating learning with positive emotions, we created ***strong anchors*** through joyful mealtime discussions, storytelling sessions, and exciting visits to book fairs.

Repetition and pattern recognition also proved invaluable, as regularly reading rhymes, poems, and short stories helped them develop linguistic skills over time.

We embraced state-dependent learning by maintaining a relaxed and happy environment, which enhanced their natural ability to absorb knowledge holistically.

Encouragement and feedback were always central to our approach; we celebrated their efforts, even when they made mistakes, which helped build their confidence and self-esteem.

Finally, we nurtured ***creativity and expression*** by giving them the freedom to explore their ideas through storytelling, drawing, and playful conversations, fostering independent ***thinking and problem-solving***.

A Foundation for Life

Today, as I watch my daughters thrive in their special ways, I feel awfully happy that we've come so far. Parenting with intention, mindfulness, and a bit of NLP-inspired practices has been one of the most rewarding experiences of my life.

It can remind us that children don't need pressure to excel; in fact, all they need is love, support, and the freedom to grow at their own pace.

Through pages turned, your dreams take flight,
A reader's journey ignites the light.

The power of words can shape your fate,
Start with a book, it's never too late.

Part 1:
Language that Clicks

A good story doesn't end with words; it begins in the imagination.

Copy That Connects

An NLP-Inspired Approach

When I began my career as a copyeditor in 2006, I never imagined the digital world would shift so dramatically in a few short years. Back then, Yahoo Messenger was our primary mode of communication. We used it to discuss editorial changes, share ideas, and sometimes just chat about our day. I remember how excited we all were when Google Chat appeared. It felt like we were entering the future, where communication was easier and more immediate.

The real change was the rise of Google as a powerful search engine. It slowly turned into everyone's go-to source for information. Need a definition? Type it into Google. Want to check the spelling of a word? Google to the rescue. Over time, this became second nature for so many people that we even turned "Google" into a verb. We were taught that search engine technology would shape how the world consumed information, and it certainly did.

During those early years, SEO (Search Engine Optimization) was still in its formative stages. The concept itself was simple: if you wanted your content to appear on the first page of search results, you had to use certain keywords. Yet the methods for doing so often felt awkward. I recall how we were told to include the most bizarre phrases in the middle of our otherwise coherent sentences. It was as though we had to wedge puzzle pieces into spots where they simply didn't fit. Even if our original text sounded perfectly fine, we had to bend and twist it to meet a keyword quota. This made the final output sound slightly off as if a robot had inserted random words here and there.

I can't count the number of times I wrote a paragraph only to have our technical team say, "That's great, but please add the *best web design company, Houston cheap,* at the end." It usually had no logical connection to the sentence I'd just crafted. I tried to make those keywords sound somewhat acceptable, but there was only so much you could do when you had to plug in a grammatically incorrect phrase. It was a strange paradox. We were told to think *outside the box* to be creative, but we also had to fit *into the box* dictated by SEO constraints.

Despite this, I wanted to remain inventive. I was also writing creatively on websites like Allpoetry.com, Sharepoetry.com, and Storywrite.com at the time. These platforms fed my desire to experiment with language and explore narratives that went beyond the demands of SEO. Eventually, all three merged under the umbrella of Allpoetry.com, which became a hub for poets and storytellers. This dual path—technical writing on one side and pure creativity on the other—shaped my perspective. I learned that you could inject freshness into even the most restricted content if you approached it with enough curiosity and flexibility.

Over the next twenty years, I watched *Google Algorithm* updates transform the digital landscape. Each update seemed to put more emphasis on what Google called *authentic organic content*. In other words, the search engine started valuing well-written, genuinely informative pieces over keyword-stuffed articles. This was good news to many writers and editors like me. Instead of finessing awkward keywords, we could put our energy into crafting high-quality, reader-friendly content. Yet the journey wasn't always smooth or simple. We had to unlearn old habits, adapt to new standards, and remain open to innovation.

My passion for language kept growing. I wrote and edited countless pieces of content, gleaning insights into how *writing*, *editing*, and even *life coaching* connect through the power of language. Language is the common element that weaves through these varied roles, and I believe that if we master communication skills, we can thrive in any task that involves words. Along the way, I came across *NLP*—Neuro-Linguistic Programming—and I found it intriguing that most discussions about it were centred on mind reading, persuasion, or sometimes hypnosis. I understood how these topics could catch people's attention, especially after the pandemic, when many seemed to develop a deeper interest in self-improvement. However, my own focus was on how to harness *NLP principles* for language-related pursuits, specifically to sharpen *reading skills*, *listening skills*, and *writing skills*, and ultimately improve *copyediting* and *copywriting*.

I saw that few had explored the connection between NLP and

language learning in depth. The more I read, the more I realised that NLP could be a game-changer for anyone who works with words. It can deepen how we read, enhance our capacity to listen actively and refine our writing process by using our understanding of how humans naturally respond to certain patterns. It also can help us become more aware of how we choose words and construct sentences, especially if we aim to be not just correct but also persuasive, empathetic, and engaging.

Below, I'll discuss how NLP helps with each of these facets—reading, listening, writing, copyediting, and copywriting. I'll include personal observations and experiences to illustrate the principles. My hope is that you'll see how these techniques can be applied in real life, whether you're in a corporate role trying to improve official documents, or you're a poet crafting intimate verses, or you're somewhere in between, blending the creative with the commercial.

How NLP Helps in Improving Reading Skills

Reading skills are not just about scanning your eyes across a page. They involve interpreting context, recognising tones, and filtering out manipulative language when necessary.

When I first explored NLP for reading, I noticed that it taught me to pay closer attention to the emotional triggers or subtle cues hidden in the text.

One approach that helped me was called *submodalities*, where you observe how certain phrases create mental images, sounds, or feelings in your mind. If you're reading a sentence that describes a quiet, dimly lit room, you might automatically sense a hush or feel a gentle chill. NLP suggests that we become consciously aware of these reactions rather than letting them slip by unnoticed. Once we acknowledge them, we gain insight into how the text is influencing our mood or perception.
For example, I used to read online advertisements without thinking much about how they played on my emotions. Then, I tried an NLP exercise. I picked an ad that read, "Transform your life and unlock unlimited possibilities." I paused and asked myself, "What images or sensations come to mind?" I realised the word transform sparked an image of a butterfly emerging from a cocoon, and unlimited possibilities made me feel both curious and slightly overwhelmed. By being consciously aware of this, I understood how the ad was subtly nudging me to aspire for something bigger while also promising a kind of magical

outcome.

Through this lens, I learned to be a more critical reader. I could more easily see which phrases were designed to inspire hope, which ones triggered fear, and which ones appealed to a sense of belonging or exclusivity. That awareness allows me to interact with text in a deeper way, evaluating if the emotional response it evokes is something I truly want or something that's being imposed on me. I believe that reading becomes more enriching when we combine traditional comprehension with this sort of NLP-based insight.

How NLP Helps in Improving Listening Skills

Listening skills often get overlooked because people assume listening is just about hearing the words. In truth, effective listening also involves tuning in to the speaker's tone, pace, and choice of language. *NLP principles* encourage us to notice the patterns in speech so we can understand not just what is being said but how it's being said.

When I attended a workshop on communication, the instructor gave us a simple yet revealing task. We had to pair up and share a brief personal story, paying attention not only to the content but also to how our partner's eyes moved, when they paused, and where they placed emphasis. It reminded me of how NLP suggests that people often reveal their thought processes through subtle cues. If someone frequently glances upward when they speak, they might be accessing visual memories or forming mental images. If someone's voice becomes softer when they discuss a particular detail, they might be emotionally vulnerable about that point.

An example that comes to mind is when I was interviewing a friend about her experiences with remote work. She repeated the phrase, *finding a balance* while lowering her voice slightly each time she said it. I could hear a hint of weariness and see that her shoulders slumped whenever she mentioned *balance*. By applying NLP awareness, I realised she was probably struggling to juggle multiple responsibilities. That insight allowed me to respond with empathy instead of jumping to suggestions or solutions.

I learned to be a good listener. It also helped me well during client calls for content projects. Instead of fixating on my next question, I try to tune in to the client's emotional shifts and repeated phrases. It's a skill that nurtures better rapport and helps me craft content that addresses their genuine concerns. Whether in casual conversation or professional discussions, NLP-based listening helps me listen between the lines, capturing nuances that I might otherwise miss.

How NLP Helps in Improving Writing Skills

Writing skills encompass far more than grammar and vocabulary. While a strong grasp of language is important, the ability to create a connection with readers on an emotional and conceptual level distinguishes adequate writing from truly compelling writing. NLP plays an interesting role here by showing us how language patterns can align with the way people process information.

For instance, an NLP technique called *pacing and leading* can be applied in writing. You start by *pacing* the reader's current experience, describing something relatable or echoing a problem they might face. Then, you *lead* them to a fresh perspective or a new solution. This is especially effective if you're writing a persuasive piece, like a sales page or a motivational article.

I once wrote an email newsletter for a wellness coach who

wanted to encourage readers to try meditation. First, I acknowledged the stress people face by describing a typical busy morning—waking up to loud alarms, checking work emails prematurely, and skipping breakfast. Readers recognised themselves in that scenario. Next, I led them toward a quick mindfulness technique. I used calming language, shorter sentences, and gentle imagery. By the time I introduced the idea of a five-minute meditation routine, they were mentally prepared.

The feedback was overwhelmingly positive. Many who received the newsletter said they felt instantly calmer upon reading it and were motivated to set aside those five minutes. Looking at it through an NLP lens, I'd used pacing and leading to mirror the readers' daily lives and then guide them toward a new, more positive choice. This example shows that NLP-based writing merges empathy with subtle persuasion, helping you frame your words in a way that resonates with what people are already feeling and then nudges them to consider something beyond their usual habits.

NLP in Copyediting and Copywriting

NLP in copyediting might sound unusual because editing is often viewed as the process of fixing grammar, style, and punctuation. But imagine this scenario: you receive a piece of content that meets basic grammatical standards but lacks an emotional pull or a clear message. You suspect the writer's words are failing to engage the target audience. This is where *NLP-based copyediting* steps in. You read each paragraph, observing how certain lines might unintentionally confuse or mislead readers or fail to spark any feeling at all. You consider submodalities—does the text evoke vivid images, or does it feel flat? You notice repeated phrases—are they reinforcing a helpful point, or are they accidentally creating a tone of insecurity or pessimism?

Perhaps the piece is an article about healthy eating habits, but it repeatedly uses the word *struggle*. Each time you read *struggle*, you sense a drop in enthusiasm. If you're editing with an NLP mindset, you might replace *struggle* with *challenge* or *journey*, words that carry less negativity and more possibility. Such subtle shifts can change the entire feel of the text, making readers more receptive to the content. You might also rearrange paragraphs so that the piece starts with a relatable anecdote, meeting the reader's mindset and gradually leading them to new ideas.

NLP in copywriting works in a similar manner but leans even more into *persuasion*, *motivation*, and sometimes *emotional appeal*. Copywriting is about prompting a specific action: maybe it's buying a product, signing up for a newsletter, or attending an event. If you've studied how humans respond to certain words or story arcs, you're better equipped to craft copy that feels both inviting and convincing. Some copywriters, for instance, use *embedded commands*—phrases that subtly encourage action. Instead of saying, "Purchase this course," they might write, "Imagine how you'll feel once you enrol in this course and discover these life-changing techniques." The invitation is woven into the sentence, leading the reader to envision themselves already benefiting from the product.

In my own projects, I've often found that an *NLP-based approach* to copywriting leads to fewer rewrites. Clients notice that the text resonates with readers on a deeper level. For instance, I worked on a fundraising campaign for an animal shelter. Rather than simply listing reasons to donate, I shared short, emotive stories of rescued animals, describing their transformation in vivid detail. The copy drew on the audience's empathy, using gentle yet urgent language. By the time I included the donation link, readers were emotionally invested. We exceeded our fundraising goal in less than a week. While good writing alone might have achieved a decent response, NLP-based writing amplified the emotional bond between the shelter's mission and potential donors.

As search engines and social media platforms grow, it's no longer enough to *stuff keywords* to get noticed. People crave stories, connections, and authenticity. That's why modern *copywriting* is a blend of strong storytelling, psychological insight, and respect for the reader's intelligence. NLP offers a structured way to practice this blend. You learn about *anchoring*, where a certain word or phrase can stir a particular feeling. You become more aware of *pacing and leading*, which helps you take the reader on a journey rather than dropping them into a sales pitch out of nowhere. You also begin to see how your tone can shift throughout the piece to maintain engagement and curiosity.

The advantage of using NLP in *copyediting* and *copywriting* is that it respects both the writer and the reader. Instead of focusing solely on grammar or basic persuasion, you're aiming for the text that truly resonates. That might mean acknowledging the reader's fears and desires, using language that gently guides them to the resolution you propose, and ensuring every sentence serves a purpose—be it building trust, sparking emotion, or simply clarifying a point.

My journey in these two areas, *copyediting* and *copywriting*, has shown me that language is indeed a powerful tool. If used clumsily, it can lead to confusion or disinterest. If employed thoughtfully, it can bring people together around a concept or a product, spurring them to act. In the past, I've had to wrangle awkward keywords and write paragraphs that felt disjointed. Now, with *authentic organic content* becoming more important, there's a greater opportunity to craft material that not only respects the algorithm but also touches the human heart.

I often think back to those early days of forced SEO, when entire phrases had to be crammed into texts, no matter how out of place they felt. Comparing that era to the present one shows how the internet has matured. Audiences have become more discerning, and so have search engines. They reward pages that provide substance, clarity, and genuine engagement. That's where *NLP-based strategies* stand out because they're rooted in understanding human thought processes and emotions. Instead of writing for a machine, we're writing for real people while still keeping an eye on best practices for online visibility.

The personal satisfaction I get from seeing a well-edited page or a well-written sales copy is enormous. It's about more than grammar or style; it's about forging a connection. Whether the topic is a new software tool, a health supplement, or an inspiring story of personal growth, the words on the page become a bridge between the writer and the audience. *NLP* reminds us that this bridge is built not only of logic but also of feelings, perceptions, and subtle cues that guide how people interpret each word.

In practical terms, if someone asks me how to get started with *NLP* for copyediting or copywriting, I usually suggest focusing on how language shapes perception. Pay attention to your choice of words. Notice if you're reinforcing an idea by repeating certain terms—positive or negative. See if you're building a journey that starts with the reader's perspective and leads them to something new. Ask yourself if your writing taps into the reader's senses or if it remains purely abstract. And, more than anything, be authentic because *authenticity* is what resonates in the long run, no matter how sophisticated the techniques might be.

As I reflect on the past two decades, I'm amazed at how *NLP*, though still not always mainstream in the writing community, has profoundly influenced the way I approach language. It has given me the tools to see beyond the superficial elements of a text. It's taught me that how we frame our words can either create a wall or open the door to a deeper connection. It has also shown me that we can incorporate seemingly incompatible demands—like *SEO requirements*—into a narrative that still feels fluid and genuine.

For anyone on a similar path, whether you're starting out as a new copyeditor, aiming to sharpen your copywriting skills, or simply exploring different ways to communicate, the key is to keep learning. As the world of content creation continues to grow and *NLP* offers strategies that adapt well to changing trends. Language has an almost infinite capacity to adapt, too. From Yahoo Messenger to real-time collaboration tools, from stuffing awkward keywords to focusing on user experience, and from mindless repetition to meaningful engagement, we've seen how versatile words can be.

My hope is that this chapter on *NLP in Copywriting and Copyediting* will inspire you to try these ideas in your own work. Maybe you'll find that your reading becomes more layered, or your listening becomes more empathetic, or your writing finds a new emotional range. Perhaps you'll spot ways to refine your editing process, noticing the small shifts in a text that change its entire tone. Even if you use just one or two techniques from the wide array that NLP offers, you might find your relationship with language evolving into something richer and more dynamic.

And that, ultimately, is why I continue to explore *NLP* in every language-related role I take on. It's not about fancy jargon or gimmicks. It's about connecting with people more deeply and conveying ideas with a clarity that resonates long after they've finished reading. I see it as part of the natural shift from writing for algorithms to writing for authentic human connection while still respecting the fundamental mechanics of digital presence and visibility.

In closing, I'm reminded of how everything started in 2006, with my excitement over Yahoo Messenger and the early days of *Google Chat*. That period felt like an awakening to the possibilities of online communication. The intervening years have brought us so much further along, and *NLP* is one of the many tools that help us navigate this evolving landscape. If you decide to explore it, you might discover, as I did, that it enriches not just your professional work but also your personal understanding of how language shapes our world.

Part 2:
Real Life, Real Lessons, Real Learning

The world she saw through tales she spun,
Her journey of storytelling had begun.

Tale of a Taleteller

Words to Weave Wisdom

Storytelling has always been a big part of my life, especially when it comes to giving speeches and lectures. Over the years, I have learned that using stories as an anchoring tool can help me connect with people in a more powerful way. In this chapter, I want to share my experiences about how storytelling can strengthen our talks, boost our confidence, and help us handle different types of audiences. I have used stories both as a motivational speaker and as a storyteller in schools and colleges, and these two roles, while similar, are also quite different. Through my journey, I have realised that developing the ability to create new stories, using classic tales in fresh ways, and involving my audience is what makes my sessions exciting and memorable. I also found that following a few simple techniques —such as asking questions, sharing jokes, and responding to feedback with humility—can transform an ordinary speech into a fun and meaningful event. By exploring these approaches and the importance of Neuro-Linguistic Programming (NLP) principles, I hope to show you how to craft and deliver stories that resonate with listeners of all ages.

My First Steps into Storytelling

When I first started giving lectures and speeches, I did not realise how powerful a story could be. I would stand in front of a crowd, usually a small group, and try to present my thoughts using facts and figures. Sometimes, it would get dry and monotonous, and I could see people losing interest. I knew I needed a better way to keep them engaged, so I started adding small examples from everyday life. These examples were not always very polished, but they were often personal and heartfelt. For instance, if I was talking about the importance of taking action in life, I might tell a quick story about how I overcame my fear of public speaking. These little anecdotes grabbed people's attention because they showed I was human. They saw that I also faced challenges and that I had real experiences to share.

As time went on, I noticed that the more I used stories, the more comfortable I felt talking to people. It was like my brain was finding new ways to link my personal memories with the topics I was discussing. Each time I spoke, I discovered new angles or bits of information that I could include. This made every talk feel fresh, even if I had presented on a similar topic before.

What also helped me was watching other speakers. I observed how they started their speeches, how they included jokes or asked questions, and even how they responded to an uninterested or confused crowd. Some of them would instantly pivot when they felt the audience was not paying attention. For example, if a speaker noticed people looking at their phones, they might pause and ask a question like, "Who here has ever felt anxious while speaking in public?" This immediately brought people back into the moment. Inspired by these observations, I practised doing the same.

Becoming Comfortable with Impromptu Speeches

Most of my motivational talks ended up being impromptu. This happened because, very often, I had to speak in settings where I did not have a lot of preparation time. Perhaps someone would call me on stage and say, "Please give us a short motivational speech on leadership." I would then look around at the audience: their expressions, their age groups, whether they seemed bored or excited. From that quick read, I would pick a story or a theme that I felt would resonate with them.

Sometimes, the topic might be completely new or unexpected, but because I have a store of experiences and stories, I can quickly adapt. For instance, if the theme was leadership, I could tell a story about how I led a small group of friends on a trip and the funny but enlightening challenges we faced. If I sensed people wanted something more serious, I could switch to a personal experience from my early career days, where I learned a tough lesson about managing a team. The key was being flexible and tapping into my own real-life moments.

In these spontaneous talks, if I found myself stuck or if the topic started to feel dull, I would switch to a question-and-answer style of conversation. For example, I might ask the audience, "What do you think is the biggest challenge for a new leader?" or "How many of you have tried to lead a group project?" When people raised their hands or started calling out answers, it breathed new life into the session. Each comment or answer gave me a fresh direction to explore.

Sometimes, a member of the audience would share a particularly interesting or funny answer. I would then build on that, adding a small anecdote or linking their response to the main point of the speech. This kept the energy alive and made the talk feel more like a dialogue rather than a lecture.

Comparing Confidence Levels Over Time

I often compare my confidence as a speaker at different ages. Once, I imagined a speaker who held a microphone at age six and then again at age thirty-eight. Certainly, a person who has been holding a microphone since childhood would have a lot of comfort being on stage. However, this does not mean someone who starts speaking later in life cannot become just as good—or even better. In my case, I only found my voice as a public speaker after many trials and errors in adulthood. Yet, by using the right techniques and learning from each speech, I found that I could face even large auditoriums without feeling my knees shake.

One technique I find very helpful is thinking of each talk as a conversation with a friend but on a bigger scale. Imagine you are chatting with one close friend, telling them a story, and seeing how natural that feels. Then, you apply that same mindset to the entire audience. Even if there are hundreds or thousands of people, treat them like a group of friends who are curious and want to hear your stories. That relaxed style can put both you and the audience at ease.

Using Day-to-Day Stories and Humor

I discovered that using day-to-day examples, personal experiences, or simple stories can help people feel more connected. For example, if I want to talk about the value of gratitude, I might tell them how I used to be annoyed by small things in life, like waiting in a long line at the grocery store. Then I would put in that I realised that I should be grateful to have money to buy food. This simple shift in mindset could resonate with listeners because almost everyone has experienced lines at the store or frustration in daily life.

Humour is another powerful tool. A light-hearted joke or a short comic tale can open the audience's hearts. It does not have to be an elaborate stand-up routine; even a small bit of fun can make the environment friendly. I like to start with something such as, "Do you ever feel like the world's biggest procrastinator? Well, let me tell you about the time I tried to schedule a gym session and ended up binge-watching my favourite TV show instead." People laugh because it's relatable. I can link that experience to the theme of motivation, showing them that I understand how challenging it is to stay disciplined.

When you use humour in your stories, remember to keep it clean and respectful. The idea is not to offend anyone but to find common ground. A short, cheerful story can be very effective. It helps people drop their guard and become more open to the topic they want to discuss.

Encouraging Feedback and Opinions

Another key technique is inviting feedback. When I give a talk, I often pause and ask the audience about their thoughts or experiences. For instance, if the session is about managing stress, I might say, "What do you usually do when you feel stressed?" or "Who here has a funny story about a time they tried to relax but made things worse?" This gets people talking and laughing. It also helps them realise they are part of the learning process, not just passive listeners.

If someone gives constructive criticism or a tricky question, I try to respond with genuine gratitude. For example, if a person says, "I don't agree with the idea of always staying positive because sometimes negative emotions are normal," I will thank them for sharing their view. I might reply: "That is a really good point, and you're right. We can't just ignore negative feelings. They're part of being human. Maybe the real challenge is learning how to handle them and not letting them control us." By responding this way, I show respect and appreciation for their input. This acknowledgement often earns more respect from the crowd because they see I am not there simply to push my ideas but also to learn and grow with them.

The Special Nature of Being a Storyteller in Schools and Colleges

When I visit schools and colleges as a storyteller, I notice how different it is from being a motivational speaker. In motivational talks, I can often rely on popular stories, well-known anecdotes, or trending topics to quickly grab the audience's interest. These might be stories many of them have heard before, and I use them as an anchor to connect to deeper lessons or discussions. But as a storyteller, my audience expects something fresh and exciting. They do not want the same fables or fairy tales they have already read in books. They want to be surprised.

To meet these expectations, I spend time reading new storybooks, exploring international authors, or coming up with my own stories. When I do use a classic, I try to put my personal twist on it or update it so that it connects with current events or today's social issues. For example, if I use a classic tale like "The Tortoise and the Hare," I might add a modern angle about the distractions of technology or the importance of mental well-being. This way, it feels different from the original version, and the moral stands out more clearly for today's audience.

Team Storybuilding with the Audience

One of my favourite activities is making the storytelling process interactive. Sometimes, I ask the audience for their favourite words and promise that I will use them in a brand-new story. This becomes a fun game. For example, I might ask a random set of people: "Give me a colour," "Give me a place," "Name an animal," "Tell me an emotion." If the answers are "purple," "moon," "elephant," and "fear," then I have to weave these four elements into a coherent narrative. It might become a whimsical tale of a purple elephant on the moon who overcomes fear to find new friends in outer space. The audience loves this because they are part of the creative process. Often, they will shout out more words or encourage me to add plot twists. By the end of the session, we have a collaborative story that everyone feels proud to have contributed to. I also promise that if I ever share this newly created story in future speeches or in any published work, I will give credit to the audience for their input. This recognition is a powerful motivator, especially for younger people. It encourages them to play with words, use their imaginations, and practice storytelling themselves.

Nurturing Creativity Through Story Games

I like to encourage parents, teachers, and students to keep playing this kind of story-building game at home or in the classroom. It does not require any special materials—just imagination and a willingness to have fun. One person can start with a single sentence, and the next person continues the story, then the next, and so on. In some cases, you can set a timer for each person, giving them 30 seconds to add to the story. This keeps the energy high and helps develop quick thinking.

This kind of exercise is not only entertaining but also educational. It improves vocabulary, fosters teamwork, and helps people become more comfortable speaking out loud. If you see a shy child hesitant to join, you can encourage them by letting them choose a simple element to include, like a favourite animal or colour. Over time, the child might become braver and decide to lead the story. For teenagers or adults, you can make the stories more complex by adding in moral dilemmas or real-world issues. This way, the storytelling game becomes a way to practice problem-solving and empathy.

How NLP Principles Support Storytelling

Neuro-Linguistic Programming (NLP) has been a great support for me in all my storytelling sessions. NLP focuses on how we communicate, how we process language, and how we can shift our mindsets to achieve better results out of what we do. In storytelling, the key is to pay attention to how our words affect the audience's emotions and imagination. I adjust my language or tone to match the audience's level of energy or interest.

If I notice that the audience appears restless, I may change the pace of my story or add an unexpected twist. If I see they are thoughtful, I may slow down, choose more descriptive language, and allow for pauses so they can reflect. Another NLP idea is building rapport. This is when you match and mirror the audience's body language, tone, or emotional state in a respectful way, making them feel comfortable. If the group is lively and joking around, I might start with a fun anecdote. If they appear more serious, I might begin with a thought-provoking question.

NLP also involves reframing thoughts. In a storytelling context, I may present an ordinary event and then highlight a lesson or a positive angle. By doing so, I help the audience see an event in a new light, a new perspective. This can be very powerful in motivational talks where the goal is to shift negative self-beliefs into more positive, proactive mindsets.

Responding to Criticism with Gratitude

Criticism is a normal part of any public speech. You might meet someone who disagrees with your message or thinks your story is not relevant. Instead of getting upset, I respond with a simple "Thank you for sharing your thoughts." This shows the audience that I appreciate diverse opinions. I usually follow up with something like, "Your perspective is valuable, and it helps me see another side of the issue." This way, I am not shutting them down or invalidating their feelings. On the contrary, I am building a bridge.

When the rest of the audience sees that I can handle criticism gracefully, they are more open to sharing their own ideas or concerns. It also makes the talk more dynamic because we might explore angles I had not thought of before. Sometimes, a critical remark can lead to a deep discussion that benefits everyone. By showing humility, I signal that I am still learning, just like they are.

How NLP Principles Support Storytelling

Through all these experiences—being a motivational speaker, an impromptu talker, and a storyteller in schools and colleges—I have grown a lot in my craft. I learned that no matter how good you are, there is always more to discover about connecting with people. I keep watching other speakers, reading books on communication, and practising new ways to include audience participation. Each speech is a chance to test a new joke, a fresh story, or a different approach to receiving feedback.

In the early days, I would become nervous if someone asked a difficult question or if the crowd seemed distracted. Now, I see these moments as opportunities to pivot. If people look bored, I might suddenly share a quick, unexpected anecdote about something in the news or something funny that happened on my way to the venue. This usually catches their attention. Or I might say, "Before we move on, does anyone here have a burning question or a funny story of their own to share?" This invites the audience back into the fold.

From Simple Anecdotes to Memorable Moments

At first, my stories were small and personal—like my difficulties waking up early or the silly mistakes I made at work. But as I continued, I realised that the more personal and honest I was, the more people connected with my words. Sometimes, I would talk about fears or failures—things that went wrong for me. People found these stories relatable, and they felt encouraged to face their own challenges.

A memorable speech often combines personal truth with a universal lesson. It is not enough to only tell a funny or sad tale; you need to connect it to a bigger message. For example, if I share about a time I messed up a project, I will also explain what I learned from it—how it taught me to be more prepared or how it showed me the importance of teamwork. This helps the audience see themselves in my story and think, "I can learn from that experience, too,"

Adapting Classic Tales for Modern Times

One of the most challenging parts of being a storyteller, especially for younger audiences, is keeping material fresh. Classics like Aesop's Fables or Grandma's old bedtime stories can be wonderful. But kids and teenagers nowadays have short attention spans, and they want to be surprised. If I choose an old tale, I try to adapt it. Maybe I change the setting: if the original story was set in a forest, I might place it in a futuristic city or on a distant planet. If the moral was about honesty, I might tie it into using social media responsibly. These changes keep the story relevant and engaging for listeners who have heard the basic plot before.

Sometimes, I invite the audience to help me modernise a tale. I might say, "Let's try taking 'Little Red Riding Hood' and putting it in today's world. How would that look?" People will suggest things like, "Instead of a wolf, maybe it's a hacker trying to fool the grandmother online." We all laugh, and then we explore how that story would unfold. This approach keeps everyone's attention and sparks creativity in a group setting.

Bringing It All Together

Looking back, I see how storytelling has shaped me. Whether I am standing before a small classroom of children or addressing a huge auditorium of adults, the methods remain similar: use relatable examples, connect through humour, ask for feedback, and adapt on the go. Storytelling allows for a more profound connection than a simple lecture does because it involves emotions, imagination, and personal experiences.

Through sharing day-to-day stories, using question-and-answer sessions, and practising meta-modelling (a method from NLP where you ask specific questions to clarify meaning), I have grown more comfortable on stage. If I feel stuck, I can shift from telling a story to a group discussion or from a group discussion to a quick anecdote. If someone criticises me, I respond with thanks and respect. This not only shows humility but also helps me learn from different points of view.

When I play a role as a storyteller in schools and colleges, I must remember that the audience is there specifically to listen to something new. They do not want old tales unless they are done in a creative way. This means I have to constantly read books by contemporary authors, create my own stories, or adapt timeless tales in a fresh manner. Sometimes, I partner with the audience to create an entirely new story using random words they suggest. This teamwork not only promotes creativity but also keeps the session lively. I encourage them to keep practising such story-building games with friends, family, or students. It sharpens their imaginations and builds confidence in speaking. Finally, NLP principles remind me to be conscious of my language and the effect it has on others. By matching the energy of my audience, pacing my speech, and reframing negative moments into positive lessons, I am able to deliver talks that stick with people long after they leave the room. Each speech becomes a shared journey, where both the speaker and audience learn something new.

It's A Continual Journey

Storytelling, whether for motivation or pure entertainment, is a continually evolving journey. Each new session, every new group of people, and every piece of feedback pushes me to explore fresh angles and approaches. I have learned to see every question—whether friendly or critical—as a chance to make the story more vibrant and to connect more deeply. Over time, the shy speaker I once was has grown into someone who can face an entire auditorium with confidence. The real secret is using techniques that make people feel involved and respected. A funny anecdote or a simple question can break the ice. Inviting people's responses can turn a lecture into a lively conversation. Constructive criticism, when met with politeness and gratitude, becomes an opportunity to learn and show humility. New stories, whether created by me or with the help of the audience, keep things fresh and exciting.

If I look back at the speaker that I was at the start of my journey and compare it to who I am now, it feels like day and night. I attribute this growth and transformation largely to storytelling. By sharing personal tales, adapting classics, and inviting people to build stories with me, I have found a way to reach listeners of all ages. I hope that by sharing these insights, you, too, can discover how storytelling might transform your public speaking or teaching experiences. Remember, it is not only about telling the story; it is about connecting with the people in front of you, valuing their input, and showing genuine enthusiasm for what you share. When you do that, any crowd—large or small—will be ready to listen, learn, and engage.

Between their laughter and silent pause,
Stories planted dreams without a cause.

Locked doors and distant faces,
Stories bridged the empty spaces.

Stories Across Screens

When the World Paused

I can't stop smiling when I look back at one of the most memorable storytelling sessions I've ever hosted. It was during the middle of the COVID lockdown that everyone was cooped up at home for months, longing for any chance to connect with the outside world. We had decided on an online storytelling session—something that felt like a perfectly simple idea at first—but, as I quickly learned, it came with its own set of surprises, challenges, and, ultimately, delightful memories.

On the day of the session, I remember sitting at my desk about fifteen minutes before the start time, fiddling with my laptop and double-checking the video and audio settings. My biggest worry was that people wouldn't show up or that we'd have a tiny crowd of silent squares on the screen. At first, that worry seemed well-founded because only a handful of people joined right at the start time. But, as I soon discovered, the interesting part of online sessions is that people tend to trickle in, often bringing their own little slice of life onto the camera —intentionally or otherwise.

Within the first few minutes, I noticed the wide variety of participants. Some had their videos turned on, looking bright, cheery, and ready to listen. Others kept their cameras off, content to just observe from the background. Then, there were a few who were so new to using online platforms that they didn't even know how to rename themselves or mute them properly. I remember seeing names like "iPhone7" or "GalaxyTab" or even a cryptic "143" that made me wonder if the participant was intentionally being mysterious or just didn't realize they could rename themselves.

Meanwhile, there was a certain comic charm in the background dramas unfolding in those little squares. People's spouses or roommates would walk by; dogs and cats would pop up unexpectedly. At one point, I saw someone's toddler wander on the screen, mouth covered in chocolate, while the parent frantically tried to get them out of the camera frame. We all giggled at the innocent chaos. But that's precisely the beauty of online gatherings: these candid, spontaneous, everyday life moments that you rarely get to see when meeting in person in a formal setting.

The Session Begins

Well, finally, it was time to start the session. I greeted everyone with a warm welcome and a big smile. I was a bit nervous, though. This was a storytelling session, after all. I wanted everyone to be comfortable and see the stories flow magically and freely. It was a mixed crowd of all ages, but I noticed that most were mothers with toddlers or kindergarteners. They seemed eager for some fun to entertain their little ones. Several older children were also present, along with a few adults who seemed to love hearing a good story. I could tell from their backgrounds—some had meticulously set up a neat corner of their home for Zoom, complete with a well-organized bookshelf or a pleasant potted plant. Others hadn't bothered about the background at all, and that was okay, too. The variety was lovely.

I kicked off the session by inviting attendees to click the "raise hand" feature (or any "I'm in" button they might have) if they were interested in sharing how they'd prepared for the session. I was genuinely curious. Was this something they had planned meticulously the night before, or did they just jump online without giving it much thought? At first, there was that awkward, pregnant pause that you often get when people are hesitant to speak up. But, sure enough, someone unmuted themselves after a moment of silence.

The First Share: A Mother's Morning Chaos

This first brave soul was the mother of a six-year-old boy. She spoke about the morning she'd had—waking up extra early, hurrying to get her child fed, dressed, and somewhat calm so that he could sit through a storytelling session. She admitted that she'd done a quick run-through with him about listening quietly, not yelling into the microphone, and even showing him some storybooks to set the mood. She said she'd been both excited and anxious. It was a brand-new experience for her child, and she wasn't quite sure how he'd behave. Would he get bored and wander off? Would he suddenly unmute and shriek into the microphone? She said it with the most endearing laugh, and I could tell that behind her words was a whole morning of miniature chaos—yet also love and enthusiasm.

Listening to her, I could see heads on the screen nodding in understanding, especially other moms. Suddenly, other people started sharing too, almost in a chain reaction, each person echoing how they'd managed to get themselves and their little ones ready for an online event. Some had turned their living rooms into mini "story corners," complete with pillows on the floor for their kids. Others had prepared snacks in advance, worried about their toddlers throwing tantrums if they got hungry mid-session.

A Refreshing 9-Year-Old Honesty

Then came a moment that made the entire group burst into laughter: a nine-year-old girl spoke up, video on, hair a bit messy, holding a cup of milk in her hand. She candidly confessed that she hadn't even brushed her teeth yet and that she was going to turn off her video every now and then to take a sip. She said it with such innocence and zero embarrassment, which made everyone laugh out loud. It was a moment of pure authenticity—she wasn't worried about looking lazy or being judged.

I asked her why she decided to be part of the storytelling session. She said she loved to be a storyteller, and her ambition is to become a story-writer one day. Her honesty, along with her big dreams, touched everyone. That instant, she unknowingly broke the mould of the "perfect participant." Suddenly, it was as though the entire session took a breath of fresh air. Everyone relaxed. Another attendee joined the honesty club and shared about him taking a quick break to answer nature's call, muting both audio and video in the process. We heard hearty laughter from the group. We'd moved from a slightly formal atmosphere, where everyone was trying to be on their best behaviour, to a more open, honest vibe.

The Beauty of Sharing Truth

I took a minute to appreciate and thank everyone for sharing these unfiltered moments of their morning. I mentioned how wonderful it was that they weren't hiding behind a façade or trying to seem "perfect." It set a warm, welcoming tone for the rest of the session, and you could practically feel the energy level rise. It was a gentle reminder that each of us has a real life behind the screen. Life can be hilariously chaotic, and it's all about how we take it. We're all human; these small real-life details make our connections more meaningful and memorable.

Introducing the Thirsty Crow

Having set the stage, I picked a very common yet timeless story to demonstrate how storytelling can evolve in the hands of different narrators: The Thirsty Crow. It's a classic tale that most of us heard as kids. I invited any of the children in the session to volunteer to narrate it. A 12-year-old girl jumped at the chance. She launched right into the plot:

> "There was a crow. He was thirsty. He found a water bottle on the roadside. It was half filled. So he picked some rocks and put them into the bottle one by one. The water level rose, and he drank the water."

She finished so quickly that it took under a minute. We all clapped—using the virtual clapping icon—and I asked her where she'd first heard the story. She said it was from her granduncle.

That revelation felt sweetly old-fashioned, reminding us how stories get passed down from relatives in our families.

Even though her version was brief, I commended her for narrating confidently. After all, no one had coached her or told her how to present the story—she just did it naturally, in her own style. Then, I asked if someone could add more details. Immediately, a 10-year-old chimed in. Her version was a bit more fleshed out:

> "Once upon a time, a male crow lived in a village. He was very active and went to the nearby town to visit his friends. On his way

> back, he got super thirsty. There was a small, petty shop where they kept a half-filled water bottle in the corner of their front yard. He tried reaching the water with his beak but couldn't. So, he flew around to find some pebbles in the garden and dropped them into the bottle one by one. When the water level rose enough, he drank the water and flew away happily."

This time, it took her a couple of extra minutes to narrate. She added a bit more flair and context, mentioning the crow's journey between two places and describing a little shop. I thanked her for the extra effort, pointing out that just a bit of extra detail can change the story into a more vivid mental picture.

A Mother's Detailed, Playful Version

Next, a mother of a four-year-old girl volunteered to share her version. Immediately, I noticed how she adapted the story as if she were telling it to a preschooler. She began:

> "Long, long ago—so long ago, I don't even know how long ago—there lived a crow in a village called Clark Town. One day, he decided to visit his friend in the nearby village,

> Cherry Hill, which was about ten miles away. After spending the day in Cherry Hill, he flew back home. By the time he was halfway there, he was so thirsty he could hardly fly. Then, he spotted a small restaurant called Red Town Grill. Next to the restaurant was a pond, and on a rock, there stood a half-filled bottle of water. The crow felt so happy at the sight of water! But the water level was too low for his beak when he tried to drink. He looked around, saw pebbles near the pond, and started dropping them into the bottle individually. After adding enough pebbles, the water rose, and he finally got his drink. Feeling refreshed, he flew back home to Clark Town with a satisfied little caw!"

We all enjoyed her beautifully narrated version, which sounded like it could be right out of a modern-day children's storybook. It was full of little details: the restaurant's name, the distance between two villages, and the crow's feelings. Then, in a playful twist, I asked her why the crow didn't just drink from the pond instead of going to all the trouble with the bottle. The entire audience burst into laughter. Without missing a beat, she quipped, "Oh, the pond was dry!"—instantly weaving a new detail into the tale.

The Evolving Story and the Power of Questions

At this point, the conversation shifted toward the idea that stories can be retold in countless ways. I joked about how, in older times, maybe there wasn't even the concept of mineral water, so would a crow really find a "mineral" water bottle lying around? Probably not. But that's the nature of storytelling—it evolves along with us. Every generation puts its own spin on the same basic storyline. Generation Y might picture the crow in a quiet, rural village; Generation X might imagine a simpler farmland setting; Generation Z might see it happening in a small city, maybe near an apartment complex or a local store; and Generation Alpha might see the crow perched on a high-tech electric pole in a buzzing metropolis. The possibilities are endless, shaped by our personal experiences and imaginations.

I pointed out how we often accept a story at face value, rarely pausing to ask questions. Yet, the moment we start asking questions, why didn't the crow do this? How come the pond was dry? Where exactly is Clark Town?—the story grows richer in detail. That's the magic of imagination. Each listener or reader brings their own mental landscapes, experiences, and creativity to fill in the gaps so the story becomes uniquely personal to each one of us.

Connecting Folktales, Creativity, and Imagination

After the crowd had warmed up with these retellings and giggles, I shared a couple of other short folk stories, each only about two or three minutes long. My aim was to highlight how the mind automatically starts filling in details—landscapes, characters, and emotions that might not be explicitly expressed through words. I asked the attendees to reflect on how each person's mental movie might differ. Some might picture the story set in ancient times, with old wooden houses and dusty roads; others might imagine modern buildings and shiny cars whizzing by. There's no right or wrong—only endless creativity.

That's where I emphasised one of my favourite quotes by Albert Einstein: *"Creativity is seeing what everyone else has seen and thinking what no one else has thought."* I also reminded them of another line attributed to Einstein, which says *imagination is more powerful than knowledge.* In my view, knowledge is what we already know or have seen. However, imagination leaps beyond that—it's the mother of invention, the spark that pushes us to dream, create, and explore.

Tying it all back to the session, I said that's the beauty of storytelling. When we read or listen to stories, It's food for our imaginations. We learn to think differently, ask questions, and picture with our minds the scenes that don't exist in the physical world. It's not just about kids. Adults, too, can nurture their creativity by engaging with stories, whether they're folktales, science fiction, real-life anecdotes, or historical accounts. And in a time like the pandemic, imagination and creativity can be healing forces, offering a mental escape from the pressures and anxieties of lockdown life.

A Session Full of Joy and Connection

By the time we were nearing the end, the audience was fully engaged. We'd started with a bit of awkwardness—people worried about being judged for not being "prepared" enough. Yet, by the end, the session felt more like a casual gathering of friends, each with a unique story, experience or perspective. The chat box was buzzing with happy emoticons and messages from people saying how they loved hearing the different versions of the same story. Everyone appreciated the warm sense of community that had developed during the pandemic times. They also mentioned that they wanted to have more such sessions on weekends, possibly to keep the momentum of creativity and connection going.

I felt a sense of deep satisfaction. Hosting online events can be tricky. You can't always gauge reactions as easily as you can in person. Sometimes, people stay muted, and you might feel like you're speaking into a void. But that day, I was reminded that with the right approach, you can create the right environment that's as engaged and playful as any in-person gathering. All you have to do is to encourage honesty, authenticity, and participation. The comedic behind-the-scenes moments, the kids' candid confessions, the parents' supportive nods, and the collective laughter all came together to form something truly special.

Reflections on NLP and Communication

At the very end, I gave a shout-out to some of the principles of Neuro-Linguistic Programming that I've been studying and applying in my coaching and storytelling sessions. NLP emphasises, among other things, the power of language to shape our realities and the importance of meeting people where they are—matching and mirroring their state of mind to build rapport by encouraging the participants to share their real, unfiltered stories of how they prepared for the session. I intended to create a comfortable space for openness. When one sees another as genuine and not being judged, it often allows them to do the same.

These small acts—the mother describing her hectic morning, the child admitting she hadn't brushed her teeth, the participant laughing about rushing to the restroom—helped strip away any formalities that might have stifled creativity. Instead, we built a friendly, supportive environment where people felt comfortable speaking, sharing, and laughing. That's an essential component of any storytelling or coaching session to ensure participants know it's okay to be themselves, stumbles and all.

Storytelling as a Seed of Imagination

In closing the session, I shared a final thought: "Storytelling is like planting a seed in the mind—a seed that, once watered by imagination, can grow into something wonderfully creative. We never know which child or adult might be inspired to write their own story or look at the world differently because they heard a tale like 'The Thirsty Crow' or any other folk story." I encouraged everyone to continue telling stories in their households, among friends, and even in random online gatherings.

Stories are universal. They travel beyond age, culture, and language and bring people together. The online session proved that a story has the power to kindle curiosity, reflection, and a sense of connection, whether we're telling an ancient moral fable or just sharing a funny incident from the morning.

The Aftermath: A Blossoming Community

After we signed off, I remember feeling a surge of energy, as if I'd just stepped off a stage to thunderous applause. The difference was that there wasn't a single stage—just a collection of small video squares with beaming faces waving goodbye or leaving appreciative messages in the chat. The best part came later, in the form of emails and texts from participants, thanking me for the session and sharing their own little spin on the story afterwards. Some mentioned that they'd retold "The Thirsty Crow" to their children at bedtime, adding even more twists. A few wrote that they were surprised at how interactive the session had been, given their previous experiences with online events being somewhat stiff and unengaging.

Over the following weeks, I noticed that my network had grown. People introduced me to friends who were interested in storytelling sessions. A couple of teachers contacted me, asking if I'd be open to doing a similar event for their class. Even some older adults who hadn't been present at the session showed interest when they heard from friends or family about what a lively time we had. It felt like the seeds of imagination had found fertile ground in more than one mind, and I found myself looking forward to the next session just as much as they were.

A Personal Takeaway

On a personal note, that session solidified my belief in the transformative power of stories. Stories aren't just for children, nor are they merely for entertainment. They are vehicles for creativity, empathy, and learning. Hearing how each participant interpreted "The Thirsty Crow" in their unique style reminded me that our minds are incredibly flexible and capable of filling in endless details, new settings, and hidden backstories. When we share stories—whether it's an age-old folk tale or a brand-new anecdote about our day—we share more than words. We're sharing a piece of ourselves, our culture, our humour, our fears, and our hopes.

Now, when I host storytelling sessions, I always encourage people—adults and kids alike—to add their personal flair. I

Looking Ahead

In the aftermath of that event, I realized I wanted to keep exploring. How could I make future sessions just as interactive, honest, and creatively stimulating? For one, I started weaving in more direct questions. For instance, if a story mentions a forest, I'd ask: "What do you think this forest looks like? What do you hear, see, or smell?" If it's a city story, I'd ask them to imagine the skyscrapers and the traffic noise. This approach makes even the most classic stories feel fresh because the listeners become active participants, co-creators of the tale. That synergy keeps everyone on their toes and ensures that no two sessions are ever alike.

I also began incorporating small challenges or prompts—like asking children to draw their version of the story right after the session or inviting adults to invent a short twist to the ending and share it in the chat. This creates a sense of community and continued engagement. Sometimes, the best ideas spark not from the host (me) but from the audience members themselves. That's another important lesson: as a storyteller or facilitator, it's crucial to step back and let others shine.

Final Words

Ultimately, that online storytelling session during the lockdown taught me something I'll never forget: Technology can't replace the warmth of in-person gatherings, but it can open doors to new, uncharted territories of creativity. We had participants from different locations, some of whom might never have been able to attend an in-person session due to geographical or time constraints. We bonded over shared laughter at each other's everyday slip-ups. We marvelled at each other's imaginative spins on a well-known moral tale. We left feeling both lighter and more inspired. And that's precisely why, at the end of the session, when many participants requested more weekend storytelling events, I was all too happy to agree. Storytelling, after all, is not a one-off event. It's a continuous journey—a path that leads us to discover not only new tales but also new facets of our own inner worlds. By embracing the spontaneity, humour, and curiosity of the online realm, we nourished the seeds of imagination within each participant, young or old.

So yes, thanks to NLP principles, open communication, and the simple magic of stories, that day turned out to be a resounding success. The Thirsty Crow might be an ancient fable, but it still gave us a reason to laugh, question, imagine, and grow. In a time when we all needed a bit of warmth and hope, a dusty old tale about a crow with a clever water trick brought together people from various walks of life. And I truly believe that those are the moments that keep us going—moments when imagination blooms, laughter is shared, and we all take a small step forward on the road to growth.

In a school where imaginations play,
Stories turned moments into a brighter day.

Sparking Imaginations Anew

Every Story Holds a Lesson

When I arrived at the school, I felt a flutter of excitement in my stomach. It was a vibrant morning, and the sky above was bright and clear, hinting at the promise of a cheerful day. When I entered the campus, I noticed neat rows of tall trees that lined the walkway, offering a gentle shade for anyone passing by. The school building itself looked both imposing and welcoming, with broad windows reflecting the early sunlight. Students in blue and white uniforms were bustling around, their voices mingling in a lively hum. Some hurried to classrooms with backpacks bouncing on their shoulders, while others cheerfully greeted friends after their winter break. In the distance, teachers guided latecomers, reminding them to get to class on time.

The principal kindly invited me to conduct a storytelling session for 6th to 10th-grade students. Children in these grades typically show a mix of curiosity, enthusiasm, and the early stirrings of teenage introspection. After a refreshing winter holiday, they often need a gentle push to return to a focused learning mode, and I hoped my stories could ease this transition. Their bright smiles and animated chatter suggested they were happy and relaxed, though still clinging to the warmth of vacation.

Walking into the auditorium, I was greeted by a delightful sight: row after row of attentive students, all eyes on me. The neat arrangement of seats and the sea of uniforms created a calming but expectant atmosphere. Teachers stood at the back, offering supportive smiles that calmed my nerves. I could hear a gentle whisper moving through the crowd, possibly students guessing what kind of stories they might hear or what activities they might participate in. Remembering my own school days, I felt a sense of responsibility to ensure they had a meaningful and memorable time.

Shifting from Holiday Mode to Learning Mode

One of the main reasons for my visit, especially after the holidays, was to *shift the students' mindset* from relaxed holiday fun to disciplined learning. Winter break often involves cosy afternoons, family get-togethers, and sometimes travel or festive activities. Returning to a strict routine can prove challenging, so my goal was to help them adapt with ease. Through storytelling—a powerful tool that gently imparts moral lessons—children can be persuaded more effectively than through direct instruction. Instead of feeling lectured, they feel entertained and subconsciously absorb the underlying messages.

Simple State Change Through Storytelling

I used what I call a *Simple State Change* to guide the students from a carefree holiday mode into a more attentive and reflective state. My approach was to begin with a short, amusing story titled "Tikki Tikki Tembo" by Arlene Mosel. This piece, set in China, introduces a boy with an extraordinarily long name who falls into a well. The tale is lighthearted, and its moral—warning against giving children excessively long names—is humorous rather than heavy. By choosing something simple and entertaining, I could coax the students into a receptive mood immediately without overwhelming them.

To enhance "Tikki Tikki Tembo," I described a vivid setting. I asked them to imagine a small Chinese village nestled among rolling green hills, with a front-yard filled with barking pups and meowing cats. I mentioned the boy's mother picking fragrant, colourful flowers in the backyard and his brother happily savouring a delicious lunch. The idea was to engage the students' senses—sight, sound, smell, and even taste. I watched them listen with growing interest, their eyes widening when I mimicked the comical moment the boy fell into the well.

Of course, the centrepiece of the story remains the boy's extraordinarily lengthy name and the trouble it causes when people try to call out for help. It's funny, it's quirky, and the moral is easily absorbed without feeling like a strict admonition. Children love tales that make them laugh, and laughter can establish rapport. When we share laughter, we form an instant bond, making it easier to build an atmosphere of trust and cooperation.

The Purpose of a Light-Hearted Opener

This entertaining anecdote was meant as an opener, a *light-hearted starter* before I dove into more substantive stories. My plan was to move gradually from humour to deeper themes, guiding them to reflect on issues like time management and personal responsibilities. When I finished "Tikki Tikki Tembo," the children's laughter and the gleam in their eyes told me they were ready for the next segment.

Introducing the Nested Loop Technique

The *Nested Loop Technique* is one of my favourite methods to maintain high levels of engagement. Instead of telling one story to completion, I open several narratives and delay closing them. This creates anticipation because listeners want to see how each story ends. It also allows me to intersperse lessons in the middle without making them feel too direct. Essentially, I lead the children through multiple layers of storytelling, weaving the core message like a thread that runs through each tale. By the time I circle back to provide closure, the message has already taken root in their minds.

Opening the Four Stories: Sarah, Tina, Mintu, and Chandal

After drawing them in with "Tikki Tikki Tembo," I introduced four fictional classmates in 8th grade: Sarah, Tina, Mintu, and Chandal. Each had distinct qualities and faced different time-management issues.

Sarah was a conscientious student, consistently topping the

class with her academic achievements. However, she focused on her studies so intensely that she forgot to participate in family gatherings or even maintain her health through physical activities. One evening, she missed her brother's birthday because she was fully absorbed in her homework. This caused deep regret when her brother said, "You never have time for me." I wanted the students to see that high achievement can sometimes lead to neglecting important relationships, highlighting the need to strike a balance.

Tina was the polar opposite: a lively extrovert who loved basketball and music. Because she was chatty, she often forgot her assignments and ended up unprepared when surprise tests popped up. The day she failed a surprise test, she feared losing her place on the basketball team. This forced her to realise that passion alone cannot sustain her future if she doesn't also fulfil her academic responsibilities. I emphasised her emotional moment of panic, hoping students would identify with that sinking feeling of being unprepared.

Mintu thrived in the outdoors, playing cricket and watching TV to relax. Yet he habitually postponed his studies, repeatedly thinking, "I can do it later." One evening, in the middle of an intense cricket match, he remembered a science project due the following day. By the time he got home, it was too late for quality work. His teacher's disappointment and remark—"Talent isn't enough if you don't respect deadlines"—stung him. Students often relate to this scenario, understanding the embarrassment of missing deadlines due to procrastination.

Chandal was quiet and introspective, lost in her realm of poetry and stories. She found so much joy in writing that she neglected her academic tasks, often remembering them at the last minute. One late night, scrambling to finish her English assignment, she realized her creativity suffered when she was pressed for time. She felt frustration and disappointment, realizing that if she had managed her schedule better, she could have both excelled academically and nurtured her passion.

The Central Message

I had now opened four-story loops—each incomplete yet interconnected by the shared theme of time management. Before resolving these narratives, I paused to ask the students, "Have you ever neglected something important because you were too busy with something else?" To my delight, many hands shot up. A few bold volunteers shared their experiences of missing a cousin's birthday or forgetting a homework deadline. Their peers responded with knowing nods, realizing they weren't alone in facing such dilemmas. This collective admission set the stage for exploring the deeper lesson that time is precious and that we must use it wisely.

Closing the Loops

Returning to the fictional classroom, I described a turning point in these four students' lives. A week later, their teacher, Mrs. Nair, announced a class debate on time management. Standing before their peers, each of the four confessed their struggles. Sarah spoke about her guilt for forsaking family events, Tina lamented her lost academic standing, Mintu recounted his failure to meet deadlines, and Chandal admitted her assignments suffered when she wrote poems all evening. Mrs Nair then summed it all up with a powerful reminder that "time and tide wait for no one." While hard work and passion are commendable, without proper planning, even the noblest goals can be derailed.

Each character then chose a path to improvement. Sarah created a timetable that included family moments. Tina decided to set limits on her talking during study periods so she could keep both her academics and her sports on track. Mintu made a point to finish homework before heading out to play. Chandal began dividing her evenings: part for homework, part for writing. This concluding set of changes resolved the stories and illustrated that time management doesn't mean giving up personal interests; rather, it means organising activities to accommodate priorities.

The Audience Engagement and Personal Stories

Watching the students' faces, I sensed how these stories resonated with them. They saw reflections of their own habits or those of their friends. I then invited them to share personal instances of missing out on important events or feeling stressed by last-minute rushes. Several brave children stepped forward. One boy confessed that he had once skipped a family function to play video games, only to regret it later. A girl admitted how chatting online with friends made her forget to study for a quiz. Their candidness lifted the auditorium's energy. The teachers at the back nodded in approval, encouraged by the interactive and honest atmosphere.

The Liveliness of the Auditorium

By now, the auditorium had come alive with an air of excitement and camaraderie. Students whispered among themselves, eager to discuss their own anecdotes, while the teacher volunteers guided them to maintain order. I felt that my primary objective—establishing engagement and rapport—was accomplished. The children no longer seemed like a passive audience; they had become active participants. We had formed a community of learners where experiences were shared openly and insights were drawn collectively.

Although the main stories about Sarah, Tina, Mintu, and Chandal were the backbone of the session, I added a few brief anecdotes to reinforce the value of discipline and helping others. For instance, I narrated how two best friends overslept and missed a long-awaited school field trip, underlining how poor planning can rob us of special moments. Each short, humorous example prompted more laughter and nods of agreement. By this time, the children were not just listening; they were absorbing, analyzing, and relating each moral to their own lives.

More Stories and Key Takeaways

As the session drew to a close, I summarized the lessons we had touched upon. I stressed that discipline is important whether one loves music, sports, art, or academics, and that managing one's time is essential for excelling in any endeavour. I also reiterated how vital it is to help others and build strong relationships—goals are more easily met when we are well-organized. The principal then graciously thanked me and praised the lively discussion. She remarked that she had rarely seen the auditorium so engaged, with such wide-ranging participation from the students.

Reflecting on the Use of NLP Techniques

When I stepped off the stage, I felt the warmth of satisfaction. My mind turned to the Neuro-Linguistic Programming techniques I had woven into the session. Reflecting on what I had done, I recognised the methods I had applied to make the storytelling particularly effective. I created rapport by speaking in a friendly, animated manner, using humour and relatable stories to connect with the students' holiday mood. This is crucial in NLP, where empathy and trust form the foundation for deeper communication.

I introduced a *state change* with the "Tikki Tikki Tembo"

story, opening a loop that piqued their curiosity and shifted them from a relaxed mindset to an engaged one. Then, I employed nested loop storytelling by offering multiple narratives—Sarah, Tina, Mintu, and Chandal—without immediately concluding them. This maintained a higher level of focus because the children anticipated each resolution. Through sensory engagement, I described sights (colourful flowers), sounds (puppies barking, cats meowing), and smells (fragrant blossoms) to make the scenes more vivid and memorable.

Another strategy that proved helpful was *anchoring positive feelings* to the learning process. By mixing humor and curiosity into the stories, I made the educational content less intimidating so the students associated lessons with enjoyment. I also used the concept of pacing and leading, acknowledging their post-holiday enthusiasm before guiding them toward an academic focus. Rather than abruptly forcing them into a studious mode, I led them gently through stories they found entertaining.

When I asked direct questions, I was *eliciting responses and encouraging participation*, which gave them the chance to relate lessons to their own experiences. This alignment with their personal stories made the moral lessons resonate more strongly. Finally, the integration of learning took place when they shared personal incidents in the auditorium. They reinforced the new beliefs and habits introduced during the session by vocalising their mistakes and insights.

Personal Satisfaction and Looking Forward

Leaving the school, I felt I had done what I came for: used my storytelling skills to help these students reflect on time management, discipline, and mutual support. The lively energy, the genuine laughter, and the open admissions of personal mistakes were signs that the session had been meaningful. I firmly believe that time is precious, and children benefit greatly when they realise the power of organising their days, nurturing their relationships, and still finding room for the activities they love most.

I also recognised how vital it is to keep evolving as a storyteller. Perhaps in future sessions, I will explore even more interactive elements—like role-playing or group storytelling—where students can physically enact scenarios. With the flexibility of storytelling and the adaptability of NLP, there are countless ways to maintain engagement. The key is to ensure that the lessons remain accessible, relatable, and enjoyable so that students feel they are co-creators of the experience rather than mere spectators.

Storytelling is An Adventure

The session concluded with the principal and teachers expressing their gratitude, and I could see the spark in the students' eyes as they dispersed. They were discussing the stories and which character they identified with the most, and planning how they might do things differently in the coming weeks. Observing such animated reactions reassured me that my efforts had touched a chord. By pairing narratives with *NLP* techniques, I achieved a blend of entertainment and education that the students seemed to appreciate.

The memory of those blue and white uniforms and the chorus of laughter will stay with me. Those bright, curious faces are the reason I love working with young people. They have an openness and enthusiasm that can be harnessed through storytelling. Hopefully, in the days and months ahead, they will recall the adventures of Sarah, Tina, Mintu, and Chandal, for sure. Also the lesson that it left - *time is precious.* For me, this

The successful session is another proof of the power of strategic storytelling and the subtle art of NLP in guiding young minds toward more productive, balanced lives.

The seeds you plant, the dreams you sow,
Will shape a world where futures grow.

Part 3:

Planting Seeds of Growth

From grains of sand to golden sheaves,
The future thrives when one believes.

Cultivating Career Paths

Nurturing Nature, Growing Futures

One of my passions is giving motivational talks to school and college students. Using NLP (Neuro-Linguistic Programming) techniques has helped me connect with my audience in truly meaningful ways. One of my most memorable experiences was delivering a career talk at an agricultural college. The session was great overall, and I connected with many students who weren't bored, whereas, in most situations, they typically were.
The theme of my lecture revolved around agriculture. I pointed out its significance, the beauty of nature, and even the poetry of nomenclature. My goal was to inspire students to see their chosen field as more than a career but as a meaningful journey. To keep things engaging, I shared short stories, anecdotes, and quotes, all of which brought the message to life.

How did I begin my lecture?

"Respected dignitaries, esteemed teachers, and dear students, a very good morning to all of you. Standing here today, I feel deeply moved and honoured to address such an inspiring audience, the individuals who have chosen one of the noblest fields for their careers. Agriculture! More than just a profession, agriculture is truly a way of life.

I'm sure that selecting this field as your future involves a great deal of thought and passion. As I walked through your campus earlier, I took a close look at the surroundings and couldn't help but notice the fascinating variety of plants and herbs growing here. It's truly a treasure trove of natural beauty and resources."

— Once the greeting is done, it's most important to connect with the audience and create trust that we are truly there for a meaningful discussion.

I continued...

"Now, let me ask you all a quick question.

"Can anyone name five common herbs that you might have seen on your way into the campus? To make it easier, I picked up a few herbs during my walk and placed them in a basket right here in front of the dais.

I would love for some volunteers to come forward and identify these herbs. If no one steps up, don't worry; I have a Plan B. I'll show you the herbs one by one, reveal their names, and share some interesting benefits about each of them. Let's make this an interactive and fun way to celebrate the beauty of nature that surrounds us!"

— It just takes a minute to initiate an interaction.

When I stepped onto the stage, the first thing I focused on was building rapport with the audience. This is one of the foundational principles of NLP. I started with a lighthearted comment about the breathtaking beauty of their campus, telling them how it reminded me of my own countryside roots.

That small moment of connection set a positive tone for the session. It created a sense of familiarity and trust, making the students feel at ease and open to listening.

Anchoring Positive Emotions Through Poetry

Another NLP principle I used was anchoring, which creates a mental link between certain stimuli and positive emotions. I quoted the 12th-century Indian poet Kambar and one of his evocative poems, "The Physiography of the Lands Around." By linking poetry to the conversation, I tied their field of agriculture to literature and nature. The students were visibly engaged and inspired, and I could see their enthusiasm grow as they started associating their studies with something much larger and more poetic. To any student who's been studying something for so long that it feels ordinary and typical, bringing up the true essence of its core can wake their sleeping enthusiasm.

Reframing Perspectives

Reframing—shifting how someone sees a situation is another powerful NLP tool. I reframed how the students viewed their career choice by emphasising not just its practical importance but also its nobility. I told them how proud I was of their decision to pursue agriculture and how their work contributes to the world in invaluable ways. It was heartwarming to see their faces light up as they began to feel a renewed sense of pride in their field.

Sparking Creativity and Future Pacing

To take things a step further, I introduced creative ideas that aligned with their education. There is a wide range of job opportunities available for agriculture graduates. How to prepare them, I suggested innovative ventures like starting herbal gardens, engaging in organic farming, or even launching glamping projects and rustic bed-and-breakfasts for urban dwellers. These ideas were met with excitement, and I used the NLP principle of future pacing to encourage them to visualise themselves successfully implementing these concepts. Future pacing helps people imagine positive outcomes, which boosts motivation and confidence.

Engaging Through Stories and Exercises

Storytelling played a significant role in my lecture. I shared personal anecdotes about my childhood in the countryside and how those experiences shaped my love for nature and literature. These stories resonated with the students, making the session more relatable and impactful. They served as metaphors for themes like resilience, curiosity, and the joy of learning.

I also made the session interactive by giving the students a small but meaningful exercise. I asked them to identify five herbs they encounter daily—whether around their campus, village or even near a roadside teashop. Their task was to photograph these plants, research their botanical background, and learn about their benefits. This exercise was a classic example of chunking down, an NLP technique that breaks big tasks into smaller, manageable steps. It helped them take actionable steps toward understanding and appreciating the natural world.

Through this exercise, the students also practised sensory activity and developed a heightened awareness of their surroundings. By observing plants closely and documenting their findings, they developed a keener sense of observation. The excitement in the room was contagious, with many students pledging to take up the challenge and share their discoveries with me later.

Feedback That Mattered

At the end of the lecture, the feedback was overwhelmingly positive. Students and faculty appreciated how engaging and thought-provoking the session was. Professors commended the way I blended literature, science, and practical guidance, making the lecture both enjoyable and insightful. The students' enthusiasm and their promises to explore the plants around them were clear indicators of the session's impact. During the feedback session, I used another NLP technique, calibrating. By paying attention to the audience's verbal and non-verbal cues, I could gauge their responses in real-time. Their animated expressions, enthusiastic questions, and

and heartfelt thanks were all signs that the session resonated with them. This immediate feedback helped me reinforce key takeaways and end on a high note.

Reflecting on the Experience

Looking back, I felt immense satisfaction. Growing up in the countryside, studying literature, and now being a life coach and motivational speaker has given me a chance to connect with people from all walks of life. This experience reaffirmed my belief in the power of connection and the role NLP plays in nurturing meaningful interactions. Seeing young minds light up with curiosity and enthusiasm was, no doubt, a joy.

Using NLP for Future Talks

This experience has motivated me to integrate more NLP techniques into my future talks. For example, I plan to use pattern interrupts like surprising statistics or counterintuitive facts to grab attention. I also want to incorporate meta-model questioning to challenge students' limiting beliefs and encourage them to think beyond their perceived limitations. Additionally, swish patterns, redirecting negative thought patterns to positive outcomes, could help students overcome their fears and build confidence.

By combining NLP techniques with my love for literature and nature, I hope to continue inspiring others to build meaningful connections with themselves, their communities, and the world around them. My goal is to leave an impact, helping people realise their potential and embrace their journeys.

The earth rewards the hands that strive,
Creating futures where dreams thrive.

Amidst the quiet of a troubled land,
Stories held us, hand in hand.

Stories Across Ages

Where Words Take Flight

I'd like to share with you the time when I was invited as a guest speaker to a higher secondary school. I was to talk to students from 6th to 12th grade about improving their reading skills. As I walked into the auditorium, I could just feel their lively energy. They were smiling, chatting, and visibly thrilled because they got a chance to come out of their regular classrooms to attend this special session. Along with me, there was another guest, a Traffic Police Inspector, who was there to speak about Road Safety.

My topic was simple and very close to my heart—how to become better readers and how reading influences our imagination.

I decided to speak impromptu because I felt I wanted to go with the flow of the students' mood and vibe. When I stood on the stage, I first greeted everyone, including the teachers, the Principal, and, of course, the giggly bunches of students.

After the greeting, I introduced an "anchor," which is usually a short story to grab everyone's attention and make them curious about what comes next. This time, I shared a very popular folktale that has been passed down through generations: '**The Crow, The Old Woman, and The Fox'.**

The Crow, The Old Woman, and The Fox

The story goes something like this: Once, there was an Old Woman who made delicious vadas (a popular deep-fried snack). A crow, attracted by the tasty smell, stole one of the vadas. While perched on a tree branch, it was about to eat the vada. Then, along came a sly Fox who wanted to trick the crow into dropping the vada so that he could eat it himself. The Fox began to flatter the crow, praising its lovely feathers and melodious voice. Filled with pride, the crow opened its beak to sing and, in doing so, dropped the vada, which the clever Fox snatched up and ate.

That was the core storyline. But as I narrated, I intentionally left gaps, pausing to let the students fill in details. It was amusing to see how each student contributed something unique. Some students shouted, "The crow flew in from the east!" while others said, "No, it came from the west!" They even chipped in with their own versions of how big or small

In the end, I asked a few usual questions about the moral takeaway—like how pride can make us lose what we have or how flattery can fool anyone. But then I asked a different set of questions:

1. **Where was the Old Woman's Vada shop?**
2. **What tree was the crow sitting on?**
3. **From which direction did the crow come?**
4. **What type of Vada was the Old Woman selling—Black Gram vada, Bengal Gram Vada, or Kidney Beans Vada?**
5. **Where did the fox come from?**
6. **What was the colour of the Old Woman's dress or saree in your imagination?**

These details were never clearly described in the basic version of the tale because the story is usually told in a straightforward way. Our ancestors would share it around a fireside or in a courtyard, and in most cases, left plenty of space for the listeners to imagine the scenery as they liked. And sure enough, the answers from the students varied—*a lot*.

- Some said the Old Woman's shop was under a tree; others said it was on the roadside.
- Some were certain the tree was a banyan tree, while others

insisted it was a Mango tree or a Neem tree.

- One student said the Old Woman wore a bright red saree, while another claimed she pictured the Old Woman in a simple white saree.

No two answers matched perfectly. At the very least, one detail was always different in each student's imagination. When I saw their varied answers, I smiled and said, "Very good!" to every single one of them. Why? You see, that's the beauty of reading and listening to stories—you can fill the gaps with your own vivid imagination.

Enter Popular Animated TV Shows

Next, I moved on to another story: a famous cartoon show. The moment I mentioned the character, the entire auditorium began to buzz with excitement. Students started shouting, the famous dialogue from the show.

I asked them questions:

- "What colour is the Main Character's hair?"
- "What colour is the outfit of the Main Character?"

Instantly, in one loud chorus, nearly everyone shouted the answers. Even the younger students who mightn't have watched the show still knew the iconic colours. Their answers were uniform and matched perfectly. Unlike the story of the

Crow, the Old Woman, and the Fox, there was no disagreement.

Why Are Imaginative Stories So Different From Cartoons or Movies?

I then asked them about the difference between the two stories. "Why did all of you have different answers for the Old Woman's story but the same answers for the Cartoon Character?"

The students thought deeply for a moment. Some raised their hands and said, "Because the Cartoon Character is shown on TV, and we can see what colour dress they are wearing!"

Another student pointed out, "In the crow story, we only have words. We don't know the colour of the Old Woman's saree or which tree the crow sat on."

This was the perfect opening for me to discuss the importance of reading stories. When you *read* or *listen* to a story that isn't accompanied by pictures or animation, your mind is free to make its own mental pictures. You become the director, the costume designer, and the set decorator all at once. Your imagination is like a blank canvas where you can paint with your own colours and shapes.

However, when you *watch a cartoon, TV show, or a movie,*

every detail is already decided by someone else. The characters' voices are fixed, their clothes are chosen, the setting is built to look a certain way, and the story moves at the pace the director sets. Your mind doesn't have the same freedom to imagine alternative scenarios. You see and accept the images that are presented to you, with typically less room to ask: "*What if?*"

How Reading Encourages Creativity

Reading is like opening a door to a secret garden that you can decorate in any way you like. When an author says, "The old woman was sitting by her shop," you might imagine a small wooden stall with a clay oven, or you might picture a modern shop with a colourful signboard. When the story mentions the crow's "deep, cawing voice," you might imagine a large black crow with shiny feathers or a skinny crow with patches of grey. Each reader's mental picture becomes unique because we bring our own life experiences and creativity to the story.

This creative process is vital for our *cognitive development.* Studies have shown that when children read stories or listen to them without pictures, they become better at understanding other people's perspectives, and they learn to problem-solve more creatively. It helps them build empathy, too, because they imagine themselves in different situations and emotions, which you may call 'putting oneself into someone else's shoes'.

On the other hand, *watching* too many videos or movies can sometimes limit that expansive imagination. Of course, movies and cartoons are entertaining, and they can be wonderful in their own way. They can showcase visual effects and storytelling techniques that spark interest in children. But when it comes to deepening your creative muscles, *reading* generally gives you far more exercise.

The Role of Questions

After I explained this difference, I took a moment to show the students the power of asking questions. In the Crow and Old Woman story, I asked specific questions to prove that the narrative was incomplete in detail. Well, those questions made the students fill in the gaps, and their creativity went wild in that process.

When you are *reading*, you naturally end up with questions in your mind like:

- "Why did the Old Woman sell vadas?"

- "What must her life be like?"
- "Could the Fox have tried a different trick?"

In a cartoon show, you still might ask questions—"Where is the Main Character going next?" or "What will happen to them?"—but visually, there's less to imagine because the show already draws the colours of the surrounding and even the expressions on their faces.

The Human Touch in Storytelling

Storytelling has been a part of human culture for thousands of years. Families once gathered around the fireplace in the evenings, sharing stories that were passed from generation to generation. These stories didn't come with movie screens or projectors. They were crafted by voice, gestures, and a few descriptive words. Listeners created the images in their minds, making each story personal and unique.

This human connection in storytelling is powerful. You can feel the warmth in a grandparent's voice as they describe a magical land. You can see the flicker of a smile when a parent recalls a tale from their own childhood. Even teachers in classrooms create special bonds with students by reading books aloud and asking them to imagine and respond.

Why Reading Matters in Everyday Life

Reading isn't just about fun or creativity; it also has practical benefits. For instance, when you read, you learn new words and get exposed to different writing styles. This improves your *vocabulary* and your overall communication skills. You start to express yourself more clearly in speech and writing.

Reading also deepens your understanding of the world. You can learn about different cultures, distant lands, historical events, and scientific discoveries, all through the pages of books. You develop critical thinking skills by comparing what you read with your own experiences and deciding what makes sense to you.

Moreover, reading can be very relaxing. It can take you away from daily stress, allowing you to enter a world of imagination or learn something fascinating. You can read on a quiet afternoon, under a tree, or curled up in bed at night. Unlike watching a screen, which can strain your eyes and keep your brain over-stimulated, reading often has a calming effect.

How to Develop Good Reading Habits

Well, developing good reading habits starts with *small, manageable steps*. I checked with many readers, and I confirmed that it works. One of my friends started out with a comic strip from the newspaper, and now she is a voracious reader. If you're not used to reading, begin with short stories or articles that truly interest you. As you grow more comfortable, gradually move on to longer books that capture your imagination. It's also important to *pick topics* you love—whether it's fantasy, adventure, comics, or science fiction, choosing books you enjoy will keep you motivated to read more.

Making *reading a routine* can help as well. Try to set aside 15-20 minutes each day for reading, whether it's before bedtime or after finishing your homework. *Discussing* what you read with friends or family can also deepen your understanding and keep you engaged. Share your favorite parts of a story or the ideas that excite you; these discussions often spark fresh perceptions. Also, keeping a *vocabulary journal* is a great way to enrich your language skills. Write down new words you come across, look up their meanings, and use them in sentences. Over time, you'll be amazed at how much your vocabulary and confidence grow.

Balancing Screen-Time and Reading Time

In today's digital world, it's nearly impossible to avoid screens, and we age quickly. We get access to age-inappropriate things easily. We lose our innocence in no time at all after having access to stuff beyond our age. In the '80s and '90s, time rolled so very slowly for us. We did chores at home, helped our grandma and grandpa in the garden during weekends, and played outside most of the time. We dealt with nature and played in the mud. We cherished each moment so in detail.

As we have smartphones, tablets, laptops, and TVs all around us these days, time rolls so quickly. We hardly have good days to remember in a year while adding another candle to our birthday cake. Gadgets eat away at our time. We don't know how days pass by.

They are convenient tools for learning and entertainment. But to keep your imagination and critical thinking skills sharp, it's important to *balance* your screen time with your reading time. If you spend an hour watching a movie or scrolling through social media, balance it out by spending some time with a good book.

Why not read an eBook instead of watching videos? eBooks can still activate your imagination because you have to visualise the scenes described in the text.

So, it's important to use technology wisely. There are many apps and websites that encourage reading, such as digital libraries and storytelling platforms. These can be great ways to explore new authors and genres.

The Joy of Shared Reading

Reading does not have to be a lonely activity. You can read together with friends or in book clubs. You can share books with your siblings, taking turns reading chapters aloud. Teachers can encourage students to perform short skits based on stories they've read, which promotes teamwork and creativity.

When many people read the same story, it's interesting to see how everyone's imagination differs. Even though the same words are on the page, each person's mental images are unique. This can lead to lively discussions about the characters' personalities, the possible hidden meanings, or how the story might change if certain elements were different. Such discussions deepen your understanding of the text and sharpen your interpretative skills.

Reading Beyond the Classroom

This is my favourite part. One of the best habits you can develop in your student life is learning to read not only for assignments but also for pleasure. School textbooks are important, but exploring the world beyond them is equally important. If you want to broaden your horizons, pick up books on subjects you don't necessarily study at school—like astronomy, mythology, historical fiction, or even cookbooks that teach you about different food cultures and heritage. Reading beyond the classroom also helps you discover new passions and interests. Who knows, you might stumble upon a topic that fascinates you so much that it becomes your future career or a lifelong hobby. Reading widely makes you a more well-rounded person, capable of understanding various viewpoints and engaging in deeper conversations.

The Lasting Impact of Imagination

The session with the students at the higher secondary school ended on a high note. I reminded them that the next time they pick up a book or listen to a story from their grandparents, they should embrace the power of their own imaginations.

Remember how they had different answers about the Old Woman's shop or the colour of her saree, while the cartoon character's outfit was universally agreed upon? That's the magic of imagination in reading.

Your imagination is like a muscle—if you use it more often, it grows stronger. One of the best ways to strengthen this skill is through reading. As you read different types of stories and books, you'll find yourself thinking about new possibilities, maybe even rewriting parts of the plot in your own mind. This sense of freedom, of "What if?" is exactly what fosters *innovation* and *creativity*.

In the future, if you become a scientist, you'll need to imagine new solutions to problems. If you become an entrepreneur, you'll need to dream up new products or services. Even if you take up a simple hobby like gardening, you'll want to be creative in how you arrange your plants or choose your seeds. Imagination affects every aspect of life. Reading is a timeless, accessible way to keep this imagination alive.

Conclusion: Embrace the Power of Reading

As I closed my talk, I could see the gleam in the students' eyes, and I felt confident that they understood the core message. Reading has the power to make you more imaginative, more thoughtful, and more creative. It helps you see the world in different colours and shapes rather than in a straight line.

Stories like **"The Crow, The Old Woman, and The Fox"** are a reminder that without a fixed visual representation, our minds can paint endless possibilities. Cartoons (or TV shows

So, the next time you find yourself with a moment to spare, pick up a book. Let your mind wander in the landscapes those pages describe. Feel the excitement of wondering what comes next. Let the faces of the characters and the colours of their clothes form in your imagination. It's your own personal movie—and the best part is, you get to direct it!

Although I didn't explicitly label the techniques during the talk, many Neuro-Linguistic Programming (NLP) principles naturally guided how I structured and delivered the lecture. Below is a summary of those principles and how they were reflected in the session:

Anchoring with a Short Story

I began by telling a short, well-known story about the Crow, Old Woman, and Fox. This story acted as an anchor for the students' curiosity and attention. Every time I referred back to the story or its details, it reignited their engagement.

Pacing and Leading

It's about meeting the audience where they are—acknowledging their current state and gradually guiding them to a new or desired state. Initially, I acknowledged the students' excitement and willingness to break free from regular classes. That was the "pacing." Then, I led them to a deeper understanding of how reading can enhance creativity and imagination, which was the "leading" part.

Utilising Curiosity with Open Loops

Open loops and questions were used to create curiosity, prompting the audience to pay attention until they came up with an answer. By asking unusual questions about the story like – Which direction did the Crow come from? I created small "open loops" that the students needed to resolve by thinking creatively, thus pulling them deeper into the conversation.

Embedded Questions and Suggestions

NLP suggests that questions and suggestions can be embedded within a narrative to direct the audience's thinking without them feeling pressured or defensive. When I asked them about the color of the Old Woman's saree or the type of vada, these questions were embedded into the story, so the students naturally explored their own imaginations. They didn't feel tested or judged; they simply became curious and creative.

Visual, Auditory, and Kinesthetic Language

Using sensory-based language helps the audience create mental pictures, hear sounds, or feel sensations, making the experience more engaging. I described the texture of the vada, the Old Woman's setting, and the crow's environment, encouraging the students to visualize the story. This approach goes for visual learners, while describing tastes and smells can appeal to kinesthetic learners, and the storytelling tone helps auditory learners.

Metaphors and Storytelling

Stories and metaphors are powerful tools to convey lessons without direct lecturing. The entire talk on reading vs. watching was built around the metaphor of a simple folk tale and a well-known cartoon character. Each aspect of the story functioned metaphorically to illustrate the difference between using one's own imagination and having visuals provided.

Reframing the Perspection

Reframing involves changing the way a situation or concept is perceived, thus altering its meaning. I reframed the students' different answers about the crow story not as "mistakes" or "confusions" but as evidence of their individual creativity and the power of imaginative thinking.

Positive Reinforcement

Offering praise or acknowledgement when people participate or share ideas encourages further engagement. After every student's answer, I said, "Very good," or "Thank you for sharing," which helped maintain a supportive environment where students felt safe to express themselves.

Chunking - From Big to Small

Moving between specific details and broader generalizations. In NLP, chunking can involve going from large concepts to smaller steps or vice versa. I started from a big idea—reading fosters imagination—then moved into *specific* details of the crow story, and finally expanded back into the bigger context of *why* reading is important and how it surpasses watching a screen for creativity.

Future Pacing

I used future pacing to help individuals envision themselves applying new insights or behaviors in upcoming situations. By challenging the students to pick a story, read it, and later compare it with a movie version, I encouraged them to apply the lesson in their own lives. This sets them on a path to actively observe and practice imaginative reading.

Milton Model Elements

It's about soft suggestions and metaphors. The Milton Model in NLP focuses on artful vagueness, embedded suggestions, and the use of metaphors or stories to bypass conscious resistance and engage the unconscious mind.

The *short story* (The Crow, The Old Woman, and The Fox) is a *metaphor* for how our minds fill in missing pieces of information. I used *soft suggestions* like "Reading makes you think and helps you imagine..." which gently leads the students to accept the positive value of reading without explicitly demanding they do so.

Bringing It All Together

These NLP principles helped shape the lecture into a dynamic, engaging session. The heart of my talk—the difference between reading (open to the imagination) and watching (visually fixed) —resonated with the students because it was presented in a way that *invited participation* and *validated their personal experiences*. Rather than simply telling them, "You should read more," the session allowed them to discover firsthand why reading might be more rewarding or intellectually stimulating than they had realised.

In conclusion, the lecture wasn't just about recounting an old folktale or mentioning a popular cartoon. It was about *experiencing* the magic of imagination. The students saw how varied their interpretations could be when a story had no visual blueprint and how uniform their memories were when referring to a cartoon that dictated every detail. That very contrast anchored the core lesson: reading lights up the mind in ways no screen can fully replicate.

By the end of the session, the students understood that every story is like a seed. If it's planted in the soil of your imagination, it can grow into a unique garden with flowers and colours only *you* can see. But if the story is fully bloomed for you on a screen—every petal, every leaf already crafted—the sense of wonder might be less intense. They left the hall with bright eyes and a renewed interest in exploring books, stories, and the limitless possibilities of their own minds.

And that is the ultimate gift we can give young readers: *the power to dream*, the courage to create, and the confidence to create, and the confidence to know that in the realm of their imaginations, anything is possible.

Final Thoughts

During the lecture, several NLP strategies naturally come into play, such as *anchoring* excitement and curiosity through a familiar story, *pacing* and *leading* the students' mental journey, and *employing questions* to stimulate internal representations and comparisons. Additional techniques include *highlighting sensory-based details* and *submodalities* to deepen engagement, using *soft suggestions* and *metaphors* (in line with the Milton Model), and reframing differences in perception as a positive outcome of imagination. By building rapport through validation and encouragement, I used chunking from the specific (the crow story) to the broader value of reading and finally provided *future pacing* to reinforce the habit of reading and imagining in everyday life.

In essence, the lecture underscores the value of open-ended storytelling as a way to encourage imagination, creativity, and personal insight—key outcomes that align well with NLP's core focus on how language and thought processes shape our experiences.

Screens and substances may cloud your mind,
But clarity and freedom are yours to find.

Leave behind what drags you low,
Rise above and let your true self show.

Mastering Your Choices

Standing in the Midst of Change

I had the chance to speak to the students of a Boys Polytechnic College about Social Media and Substance Deaddiction. Before the session, I'd a casual chat with an advocate who was also a special guest. She planned to discuss some basic laws every student should know.

During our conversation, I learned that a few students from the college had been involved in substance exchange and had even visited the police station because of addiction issues. We often see news and videos about this kind of reality, but meeting these students face-to-face and knowing they're caught up in it was quite shocking. Initially, I intended to focus mainly on social media and smartphones, only briefly touching on substance de-addiction. But after hearing about the situation, I decided to give both topics equal importance since they're closely connected.

When I looked at the audience, they were all so young, around 18. Some students looked so innocent, and I felt sad knowing that a few among them had already been exposed to the darker side of society. Still, I believe that we can help them change. I was determined to reach their minds with the right words in the right way. They should know about the beauty of life and how these distractions would ruin their future.

I saw many awards and trophies lined up on the shelves of the auditorium. They had beautifully displayed the trophies to show that many students had excelled in academics and sports, bringing home numerous prizes. It made me think more carefully about connecting with them and guiding them toward making wise choices.

Once I started speaking, I asked them simple questions about their goals, career plans, and hobbies. They came up with very interesting answers. Some students wanted to pursue higher studies, while others planned to work part-time while continuing their education. As our discussion was already focused on goals and careers, I introduced a true story about two friends I know, hoping it would inspire them.

Shyam and **Daniel**. Both hailed from a small countryside village and attended the same school. After completing their schooling, they moved to a nearby city to pursue engineering. After graduation, they both secured jobs in a metropolitan city. Despite their similar beginnings, their paths in life turned out very differently.

Shyam's Journey

Shyam was the brighter student among the two, a first-rank holder. He secured a slightly better position than Daniel in the same multinational company. Though both started at L6 positions, Shyam was more ambitious and curious about city life. He quickly adapted to the trendy and fast-paced lifestyle of his city-bred colleagues. He upgraded his wardrobe, bought a fancy wristwatch, and frequented fancy restaurants and coffee clubs. He tried his best to fit into his new social circle.

Initially, Shyam was successful in all his efforts. He bought a plot of land in his village, built a grand house, and hosted an extravagant housewarming ceremony. His relatives and friends praised him for his quick success. However, his desire to please others led him down a dangerous path.

To impress his city friends, Shyam started visiting upscale international cuisine restaurants. Gradually, he began adopting habits he had never engaged in before. In social gatherings, he started drinking. What began as casual drinking soon turned into addiction. The more he drank, the more his performance at work deteriorated. He received a warning letter from his manager and was eventually demoted. A year later, Shyam lost his job and found himself in a rehabilitation centre. He isn't married yet. He is depending on his parents for support now. How sad it was to see a successful man fail miserably in his life.

Daniel's Journey

Contrarily, Daniel chose to remain grounded, even though he wasn't a topper like Shyam. He focused on his work, earned good, and built a modest house in his hometown for his parents. At the same time, he stayed close to his friends, who respected his simplicity. He never felt embarrassed about his roots in the countryside. He always felt proud of his identity. He often talked about the benefits of living in a peaceful environment full of fresh produce, farmland, cattle and open spaces close to nature. He would even go all out to invite his friends to spend weekends at his place, giving them a little taste of a calm and quieter life. Over four years, Daniel developed a tight-knit circle, making lifelong family friends.

Even when he visited the city, Daniel stuck to his choices

without letting anyone pressure him into changing just like that. His stable approach to life paid off, and he married someone whose values matched his own. Together, they built a happy and secure life. I saw the full picture of Daniel's journey at his wedding. No one seemed to have any negative opinion about his successes. At the same time, people were also discussing how Shyam failed in his life after getting addicted to his drinking habit. They were concerned and hoped he would eventually find his footing.

As I stood there, watching Daniel surrounded by love and genuine friendship, I felt many emotions—sadness for Shyam, admiration for Daniel's grounded attitude, and hope that things might still change. Daniel continued to express his wish for Shyam to recover. The contrast between these two friends reminded me that success in life isn't defined just by wealth or bank balance. Living a life with a city's comforts doesn't define success if one can't stay true to oneself and make meaningful relationships. Even after so many years, Daniel stays humble and hopeful, ever grateful for the simple joys of life. He values his friends no matter what without changing his choices.

The Students' Reactions

Sadly, when I finished narrating the story, I noticed a few students nodding their heads in agreement with what I shared. Some students even shared personal stories about family members who had suffered failure because of addiction. They shared about how abusive their fathers were and how their families were affected emotionally and financially. Their eyes speak more about their pain than their words when they opened up. It was both heartwarming and heartbreaking to listen to.

We discussed how substance or alcohol addiction could derail a person's life. I insisted that a person's addiction not only harms the concerned individual but also affects their family members and loved ones. They lose their life, break good relationships, and lose good opportunities.

Moving to Smartphone De-addiction

The discussion slowly moved to the topic of smartphone addiction. I encouraged the students to share their thoughts about the positive and negative aspects of modern gadgets and smartphones.

Some students spoke about how smartphones are helpful in daily life. They talked about how easy it is to access current information, stay connected with friends and family, and use apps to learn new skills or for educational purposes. They highlighted how technology has made life easier and more productive.

Some of the other students discussed the darker side of smartphones. They shared their thoughts on how social media apps can be dangerously addictive and cause people to spend way too much time scrolling for what feels like forever. Certain online media can affect one's self-esteem by making them compare themselves to others—in most cases, strangers. Many admitted that too much screen time distracts them from focusing on their studies and other important activities.

I repeated something I'd previously shared in a motivational talk with a different set of school students: "We age so quickly these days because of smart gadgets. We don't have time to think for ourselves and often let others take up our time. Most of our time is spent watching others do the things we enjoy. It isn't good and can harm the younger generation, who are losing out on proper sleep routines." I explained how poor sleep habits affect their health and why we need to focus on making ourselves a balanced lifestyle. It brought us to the important idea of maintaining a

"Sound mind in a sound body." I emphasised the importance of following a healthy diet and sleep routine.

We slowly moved on to discuss how to maintain a work-life balance. I explained that it was not about avoiding gadgets entirely or using them all the time. If they choose either extreme, it will be harmful, I emphasised. I advised them to use the gadgets mindfully to strike this balance.

The students also came up with their ideas and tips. I suggested that they set time limits for social media usage. I encouraged them to choose real-life interactions with friends and family over virtual ones on social media platforms. I also emphasised the importance of using technology as a tool for growth, not as an escape.

The students actively participated in brainstorming ideas to help themselves and their friends manage smartphone use better. They came up with creative suggestions like organising outdoor activities, forming hobby groups, or planning group study sessions as alternatives to excessive screen time.

I reminded them that smartphones are powerful tools, but they should work for us—not the other way around. By being mindful, they can still enjoy the benefits of technology while staying healthy, focused, and connected to the real world. The energy and determination in the room gave me hope that these young minds would make positive changes— not only for themselves but also to inspire their peers to do the same.

I reminded them that smartphones are powerful tools, but they should work for us—not the other way around. By being mindful, they can still enjoy the benefits of technology while staying healthy, focused, and connected to the real world. The energy and determination in the room gave me hope that these young minds would make positive changes— not only for themselves but also to inspire their peers to do the same.

How NLP comes in here

In this story, NLP is woven into the narrative in subtle ways. *Anchoring* was used when Daniel's countryside background became a positive point of reference that kept him stable. *Reframing* occurs when he proudly embraces his roots, turning what some consider a drawback in status.

There's also *sensory-based language* in the mentions of fresh food and calm surroundings, which engage our senses and evoke a peaceful mood.

Meanwhile, *pacing* and *leading* gradually shift focus from Shyam's struggles to Daniel's steady progress, guiding us to notice the value of staying true to one's identity.

And there's a hint of *future pacing* in Daniel's happy marriage, suggesting that a fulfilling life follows from full-of-heart and healthy choices. By putting all this together, the story subtly tells how consistent values, strong self-belief, and an appreciation for one's background can set the path for a stable and meaningful life.

The lecture on smartphone addiction incorporated several *Neuro-Linguistic Programming principle*s to make the discussion engaging and impactful. One key principle was *building rapport* with the audience. By encouraging students to share their experiences and thoughts openly, I created a safe and inclusive environment where everyone felt comfortable participating. This approach helped establish trust and connection, which are great and needed for meaningful communication.

I used *anchoring* once again by using a phrase from a previous lecture: "We age so quickly these days because of smart gadgets." This emotional anchor triggered awareness and reflection among the students. With that statement, I wanted to reinforce the importance of striking a balance with technology. Their poor sleep routine, tendency to compare themselves with others, and tendency to follow or copy others make them lose who they are. This thought further deepened the tone of the anchoring idea.

The principle of *chunking information* was also applied to make the content easy to understand and absorb. I broke down the discussion into manageable parts by looking at both the *positive* and *negative aspects* of smartphones. From easy access to information and skill-building to addiction, distraction, and social comparison, students processed the final say bit by bit, easily relating to and internalising the ideas.

Through *reframing*, I shifted the students' perspective on smartphone usage. Beyond the positive and negative sides of the gadgets, I guided them to see it as a tool that can either support or hinder their growth, depending on how it is used. For example, I encouraged them to focus on *mindful usage* by setting time limits, prioritizing face-to-face interactions, and using technology for skill-building rather than as an escape. This shift in perspective helped them see the importance of balance in a new light.

The brainstorming session also introduced the principle of *future pacing*. I asked the students to imagine how their lives could improve if they applied the strategies we discussed to organise their lives with outdoor activities, planning group study sessions, and reduce screen time, and to imagine a more positive and balanced future, making the solutions attainable and motivating them to act.

In the end, the *sensory language* I used made the lecture more engaging and relatable. I explained how the *tangible effects* of excessive screen time would take an *emotional toll* on their life and make them miserable.

The lecture was informative and empowering by combining the NLP principles of *building rapport*, *anchoring*, *chunking*, *reframing*, *future pacing*, and sensory *language*.

I insisted that healthy routines and meaningful habits will surely help them change their lives for good in many ways.

We ended the session on a hopeful note. I encouraged the students to take charge of their lives and make choices that align with their goals. We agreed that the present moment is precious and that building genuine relationships and experiences is far more rewarding than any short-lived high from substances or virtual validation.

The advocate who shared the stage with me as a guest lecturer also shared his thoughts about the importance of following rules, discipline and self-care routine. Together, we left the students with actionable steps and the motivation to make better choices for themselves and their communities.

I left the college that day feeling at ease, knowing that we had sparked meaningful conversations that definitely might inspire positive change.

A healer's path demands precision,
Time's mastery fuels your vision.

Every Second Counts

In medicine and in life's domain

I remember the day I visited a well-known Medical College to give a motivational lecture on the importance of time management. It was a bright, sunny morning, and the campus looked grand and peaceful. Rows of tall trees bordered the walkways, offering shade to students in white coats rushing from one building to another. A few students chatted happily, while others looked deeply engrossed in their phones, notes, or textbooks. I felt nostalgic, as they reminded me of my college days when I, too, would juggle classes, assignments, and personal life.

When I reached the auditorium, the medical college dean who had invited me to the lecture greeted me. He was a warm, friendly person with a gentle smile, yet I could see a hint of curiosity in his eyes, as if he wondered how I would manage to connect with a crowd of tired, stressed-out final-year medical students. After all, these students were in a critical phase of their education, often described as the hardest part of their journey. And they are future doctors who are going to save lives. No doubt, they had lived through years of rigorous study, practical sessions, sleepless nights, and endless examinations. As they approached the final lap of medical school, the pressure had mounted even more. Many were anxious about final exams, upcoming internships, and their professional future.

I walked into the large, well-lit auditorium. I noticed the rows of seats slowly filling up with students. Some wore stethoscopes around their necks, some clutched thick textbooks, and others were scrolling through their smartphones. Their faces appeared dull and exhausted. Dark circles under their eyes suggested they had been burning the midnight oil, possibly preparing for their next set of exams. A few students looked happy and cheerful. Some were chatting in small groups in serious tones. Some were sharing some inside jokes and laughing among themselves. Still, the atmosphere felt heavy. These young minds were carrying the world's weight on their shoulders.

I smiled at the audience. "Good morning, everyone!" I said warmly into the microphone. A soft, collective mumble of "Good morning" returned, not quite echoing my enthusiasm.

The Medical Professor nodded encouragingly from the front row. I could tell he hoped I would inject some positivity into the students' minds.

I introduced myself briefly and thanked the college for inviting me. I said I was excited to speak about **time management** because I knew how essential it was for final-year medical students. "I understand how stressed you all can be," I said, "with your internship, examinations, and the constant pressure to keep updating your knowledge in the medical field. But trust me, you can make your life much easier if you learn to manage your time effectively."

I continued...

"Before we begin, I'd like to share a little story with you." Only a few people seemed to pay attention to hearing what I said. Many looked down at their laptops or phones. However, I knew from experience the power of storytelling and how a good story can grab the attention of the audience. So I asked, "How many of you like stories?" A few hands rose, a bit reluctantly, but it was enough to create a spark of curiosity. I said, "Let me tell you the story of a poet who was the biggest procrastinator in his kingdom."

The Poet Who Missed His Golden Chance

I started in a playful, animated tone: "Once upon a time, in a distant land, there lived a mighty King who ruled over a kingdom full of lazy people. The King was an enlightened ruler. He wanted to motivate the people in his kingdom to be more active and achieve big successes in their lives. Pondering for months, he decided to organise a grand contest, promising an amazing reward. "The contest attracted everyone in the kingdom, from farmers to soldiers, merchants to scholars.

The King made an announcement to the people, asking them to assemble at the auditorium at 7 a.m. the next day. The auditorium was filled with people. All were curious and excited to know what the contest was all about. When the King came in, the first question he asked was, "Who would like to have the key to the room of luck?"

People looked confused and didn't know how to react to this sudden question. But one person said loudly, " I would like to have the key, your majesty."

The King exclaimed, "Bravo, you are the winner! Come and take the key to the Room of Luck."

The prize was the key to the royal treasury. The winner could have the key for an entire day, from sunrise to sunset. During those hours, the person could take home as much gold and silver as possible. The only condition was that they had to be there to open the treasury door after sunrise and close it before sunset. The doors would close if the sun went down, and no one would be allowed inside.

"But the winner, in an unexpected twist, turned out to be a poet. This poet was known for his eloquence, creativity, and incredible ability to procrastinate. When the King handed him the key, the poet was overjoyed. He rushed home to share the news with his wife, who was thrilled at the thought of becoming rich.

"The next morning arrived—this was the special day when the poet could enter the treasury. But he woke up late, as usual. His wife came running to him, waving the key, reminding him, 'My dear, hurry up! Go to the treasury before the sun sets. We don't want you to miss this once-in-a-lifetime chance. Rubbing his eyes, the poet replied casually, 'Don't worry, my dear. Even if I go in the afternoon, I'll have plenty of time to grab enough gold to last us a lifetime.

"He then asked for a hearty breakfast. His wife prepared **Idli** and **Ghee Dosa** with a bowl of delicious sambhar. I could see some students laughing at the mention of their favourite breakfast dish.

I took a small deviation from the story and asked how many had Dosa for their breakfast. I was not surprised to see half of the audience raising their hands with a smile.

So, you all know how tempting Ghee Dosa with Sambhar would be. No wonder the poet enjoyed his breakfast, savouring every bite while time ticked away. After breakfast, he felt a bit sleepy and thought, 'A quick nap won't hurt.' So he dozed off again, waking only when it was close to noon.

His wife, filled with excitement about the wealth and jewels her husband would soon bring home, prepared a lavish lunch. The platter was loaded with rice, roti, dal, vegetables, papad, curd, and sweet dishes. When he woke from his nap, he sat down to eat, greeted by his wife's beaming smile. She served the meal lovingly, and the aroma of her cooking filled the room. Known for her culinary skills, she did a great job, and the food was absolutely delicious. He enjoyed every bite, eating until he felt his tummy full. After the hearty meal, he took another short nap and had a refreshing cup of tea.

His wife, now panicking, insisted,

'Please, my dear, you must go now! If you wait any longer, you'll lose this golden opportunity!'

The poet smiled and said, 'Relax, there's still a long time until sunset. A few hours will be more than enough to gather plenty of gold.'

Then he insisted on a big lunch, followed by a cup of coffee. One thing led to another, and before he knew it, the clock struck four in the afternoon.

"Finally, he set off for the palace, the treasury key in hand. Unfortunately, that day was unusually cloudy, and the sun began setting sooner than expected. When the poet reached the palace gates, the treasury guards were already locking up. 'I'm sorry, Sir,' said one guard, 'the King gave strict orders that no one may enter after sunset. You're too late.' The poet pleaded, but no use. He had missed his golden chance simply by procrastinating and ignoring the passage of time.

The poet returned home empty-handed. He realised what a foolish mistake he had made. He had wasted the entire day in laziness. This was a day that could have changed his life forever, yet he threw it all away by delaying and not valuing the importance of time.

At the end of the story, the students laughed at imagining this lazy poet's one-day day routine of eating, napping, and sipping tea without realizing how quickly the sun was setting down. It was a bit funny but also sobering. I noticed that quite a few students sat up straighter in their seats. Some exchanged smiles and knowing looks. The story delivered its message — If you spend your time chasing fleeting pleasures while neglecting what truly matters, you could miss out on opportunities that have the power to transform your life.

The Students' Reaction

I looked around and asked if anyone here feels like the poet sometimes. A couple of students giggled. Understandably, their answer was a big *YES*. A brave young man raised his hand, admitting that he often postponed his study sessions until the last minute. He added that it resulted in sleepless nights and unnecessary stress many a time. Another student chimed in that social media was her biggest distraction. She admitted that she spent hours scrolling through her social media feeds before realising the entire evening was gone.

Everyone suddenly seemed more comfortable. They openly started admitting their struggles with procrastination.

The atmosphere lightened, and I saw that the initial resistance or dullness in the audience had shifted into genuine curiosity. There, I felt a sudden-lit willingness to explore how they could change.

More Stories of Missed Opportunities

I decided to reinforce the lesson with a few more anecdotes. After all, we learn best when we see the same principle applied in various real-life scenarios.

The Boy Who Failed an Entrance Exam

I told them about a very intelligent boy who lacked consistency in his studies. He had an important Entrance Exam that could open the doors to a government medical college.

However, because he spent too much time on entertainment and social media, he neglected his preparations and didn't properly manage his schedule. When the exam day arrived, he realised he wasn't ready. He failed to secure the required marks.

As a consequence, he had to wait an entire year to re-attempt that exam. In that year, he not only faced disapproval from his family and friends but also the mental burden of knowing he had lost a whole year. This is a matter of a year going wasted. The audience seemed to be agreeing with my statement that time, once gone, never returns.

The Boy Who Missed a Train

Then I mentioned the story of a boy who missed his train by just a few minutes, thereby missing an important job interview in another city. That one job interview could have changed his life. He had spent too long saying goodbye to his friends, or maybe he had lingered over breakfast. Whatever the reason, he arrived at the station slightly late. All he could do was to watch the train chugging away in the distance. He was devastated, realising that this seemingly small delay had cost him a potentially life-changing opportunity.

By sharing these stories—starting from the poet who squandered an entire day, to the boy who lost a year, and then to the boy who missed out by mere minutes—I tried to show the audience that time mismanagement can impact us in small ways and in large ways, but the result is always a personal loss. It's all about how wisely we use our time. Right time, right space, right decision.

The Shift of Vibe in the Room

I observed the students' body language again. Their expressions had changed noticeably. Many seemed introspective as if reflecting on their own habits. I saw a few students exchanging whispers with their friends, probably discussing how they, too, could avoid becoming like the poet or the boy who missed the train. The Professor, sitting in the front row watching attentively, nodded and smiled softly.

I felt grateful for the power of stories. These stories, drawn from everyday life or from grandma's stories, hold a mirror to our own behaviours. The truth is hearing about someone else's mistakes motivates us more than being scolded or lectured about our mistakes or failures.

Diving Deeper into Time Management Techniques

Now that the stories had softened the ground, I began a more structured discussion on time management. I wrote a few points on the whiteboard:
I explained these points in simple language, with examples that medical students could relate to. For instance, *prioritisation* could be choosing to study pathology before

spending hours on social media if pathology was the subject they found most challenging. *Setting clear goals* might look like deciding they want to finish reading a particular chapter by tonight rather than vaguely telling themselves they should "study more."

It's important to *avoid distractions* if you want to stay on the track. So, it's advised to minimise or eliminate social media use during scheduled study hours. Another key strategy is *scheduling and deadlines*, which means creating a practical timetable and sticking to it to maintain consistency and accountability. Finally, practising *self-compassion* is essential.

Know that occasional slip-ups are natural, forgive yourself, and don't guilt-trip yourself. Applying these strategies helps one have a balanced approach to managing time effectively, reducing stress, and improving overall productivity while staying motivated and confident in one's abilities.

We also touched upon the **Pomodoro Technique**, a popular time management method where people work for 25 minutes and then take a 5-minute break. Some students said they had tried it but felt it wasn't flexible enough for their lengthy study

study sessions. Others liked it because it forced them to focus intensely for short bursts. We discussed the *pros* and *cons*, such as how the technique can be great for tasks that demand deep concentration, but for certain medical procedures or practical sessions, it might be disruptive to stop every 25 minutes. The key, I stressed, is to experiment and find the right balance for their personal study style.

Addressing Social Media Addiction

When the topic of social media came up, I noticed many heads nodding in agreement. A student near the front row raised his hand and admitted he often lost track of time because he scrolled through Instagram or watched YouTube videos whenever he felt stressed. Another chimed in that late-night browsing was affecting his sleep schedule and, consequently, his efficiency in morning classes. One student joked, "I think I can recite all the trending reels by heart, but don't ask me about the latest updates in pharmacology." We laughed, but there was a collective recognition of how big a problem social media can be. "Social media in itself isn't bad," I explained, "but our **relationship** with it can become unhealthy. We must learn to control our use of these platforms instead of letting them control us." We must learn to control our use of these platforms instead of letting them control us." We brainstormed practical steps:

- Switching off phone notifications during study hours.
- Logging out of social media apps or even temporarily uninstalling them during exam weeks.
- Allocating a small 'social media break' after finishing a set amount of study.

Some students offered their own tips. One shared how he used a special application that blocked social media apps for a long time so he wouldn't be tempted to open them. Another used a reward system: if she finished a certain chapter, she allowed herself ten minutes on social media. This lively group discussion, with many students contributing fresh ideas, showed that they were engaged and genuinely eager to adopt better habits.

The Role of Stress and Self-Care

I also spoke about stress management, which is tightly interwoven with time management. We often procrastinate not because we are lazy but because we feel overwhelmed. We fear the gigantic task in front of us. In the case of medical students, to the pressure to perform well in exams, handle practical cases, and constantly update themselves can become stifling. It's easier to slip into escapism when anxious—watching random videos, taking too many naps, or indulging in excessive snacking.

"The key," I said, "is to break down large tasks into manageable chunks. Acknowledge you can't do everything at once. And most importantly, please remember to look after your mental and physical health. Take short walks, speak with friends, or engage in a hobby for a limited time. Self-care is not a waste of time; it's an essential investment in yourself that helps you remain productive in the long run."

During the discussion, some of the students began sharing lighthearted, inside jokes about how they tried (and often failed) to stick to a study schedule or how they would set multiple alarms only to keep hitting snooze. One student joked about an old trick: "I used to place my alarm on the other side of the room, so I'd be forced to get out of bed. But in the morning, I'd just walk over, snooze it, and go right back to sleep!" This anecdote made everyone laugh, especially since it was a reminder that no matter how well-planned your routine might be, discipline matters just as much as scheduling.

However, the tone soon shifted as they started discussing the high stakes of *time management in the medical field*, especially in emergency medicine. One aspiring surgeon spoke up passionately: "It's not just about passing exams or finishing our assignments on time. Every second in the ER can be the difference between life and death for a patient." Another student nodded and added, "We might joke about hitting the snooze button now, but once we're in the emergency room, the concept of 'five more minutes' doesn't exist. Every minute counts."

They recalled clinical rotations where quick thinking and efficient action were crucial. One story involved a patient who came in with severe trauma; the team had only a narrow window to stabilize the patient. The student recalled, "That day, every second was precious. We couldn't afford to be slow or unsure. It made me realize that time is not just about personal productivity —it's literally a matter of patient survival."

The students also pointed out that while textbooks emphasized medical knowledge, the *practical aspect of managing limited time*—whether it's during surgeries, in clinics, or managing shifts—was something they learned more from hands-on experiences and senior doctors' guidance. The group agreed that if they could improve their everyday time management habits now, they'd be far more prepared for the challenges of high-pressure medical environments later.

These serious insights underscored *how important time management truly is* for them: not only for academic success but ultimately for *saving lives.* That reality check gave the session a deeper meaning. Their inside jokes about alarm clocks and snooze buttons suddenly took on a new significance when viewed through the lens of real patient care and medical responsibility.

NLP Techniques at Play

Though I didn't explicitly label them as such during the lecture, I employed several Neuro-Linguistic Programming techniques to connect with the audience and make the message stick:

In the session, *storytelling (anchoring)* played a key role as I began with the story of a poet who procrastinates. The story served as an anchor to illustrate the consequences of poor time management, making the message memorable and relatable. Through *pacing* and *leading*, I first acknowledged the students' stress and heavy workload, aligning with their current mindset (pacing) before guiding them toward practical solutions (leading). I encouraged *questions* and *reflections* by asking if they ever felt like the poet, which prompted internal reflection and allowed them to take ownership of the solutions being discussed. Also, I used *positive reinforcement*, frequently saying, "That's a great idea!" or "Thank you for sharing!" whenever a student contributed, creating an encouraging environment. I appreciated their willingness to participate and engage actively. Together, these strategies worked for good and made the session impactful, resonating deeply with the students. Gradually, the room's energy transformed. What began as a dull session with a reluctant crowd turned into a lively, interactive group that shared tips, laughter, and concerns. I could sense the relief they felt upon realising they weren't alone in their struggles.

Finally, A Friendly Note

As the session neared its end, I noticed that nobody seemed eager to leave, even though we had spent much time. Some students folded their arms, but they were leaning forward, eyes sparkling with interest. Others were smiling and seemed relaxed, as though a mental burden had been lifted.

I finished by saying, "Time is our most precious resource. It's the only thing that, once spent, we can never get back. Each of you has tremendous potential, and each day presents an opportunity to get one step closer to your dreams. Don't be like the poet who let the day slip away or the boy who missed his train. Embrace every minute as a gift. You don't have to be perfect, but try to be aware of how your choices today shape your tomorrow."

A soft hush fell over the room. I could see the students processing the message. Then came the warm and genuine applause. The Professor stood up and expressed his gratitude, hoping the students would remember these stories whenever they felt tempted to procrastinate.

A few students came up to me afterwards, smiling shyly. One said, "That was exactly what I needed to hear today. I have been so stressed, and I keep telling myself I'll manage my time better 'tomorrow.' But after hearing these stories, I realize I need to do it now." Another young woman mentioned how she had grown addicted to her phone due to exam stress, constantly refreshing her social media feeds. "But now," she said, "I think I will try uninstalling some apps for a few days and see how much more time I have for studying."

As I prepared to leave, I felt both happy and hopeful. These students were on the verge of beginning a new chapter in their lives—stepping into the medical field as future doctors who would be going to save lives and help those in need. The world needs dedicated doctors, and I believe that with proper time management, these young men and women could truly excel in their calling.

Reflecting on the Day

On my way back home, I recollected the entire experience. It was proof to confirm that the power of storytelling can transform even a room of people with dull exhaustion into people of active engagement. All we have to do is to quote relatable examples and a few easy yet powerful stories. The stories and discussions around the stories are just an emotional nudge to remind us that time is valuable. No complicated or sophisticated tools are needed here.

The poet's story still lingers in my mind. I visualised him dozing off in his chair, perhaps dreaming of gold, only to wake up and realise he had lost the chance to make his dream a reality. In the same way, I thought about all the times in my own life I had delayed important tasks until it was almost too late. Even

though I was the speaker today, I was also learning from the stories, reinforcing my own resolve not to waste time.
I believe each one of us has a "poet" inside—a part that enjoys leisure and underestimates the speed at which time can slip away. We also have a "boy who missed a train" inside—a voice that sometimes tells us, "It's okay, just another five minutes," until we find ourselves running desperately, only to see the train vanish into the distance. Recognising these tendencies is the first step to conquering them.

Final Thoughts

Finally, the session at the medical college was not only about listing the techniques of time management but also about breaking the stressful routine the students go through. Such a break serves as a breeze to give them time to think and reflect on their current needs and ways to achieve their goals.
It reminded me of the hard truth that how we spend our hours shapes our days and our entire lives.

Even as I left the auditorium, I could sense the lingering energy of the discussion. Students were still talking among themselves, forming small circles, revisiting the stories, and promising each other that they would try to make immediate changes in their routines. Some would fail at first, and some might revert to their old habits. But at least they had become aware of the pitfalls of procrastination and the power of seizing the moment.

And that, for me, was a mission accomplished. Suppose even one student leaves the session determined to manage their time more wisely. In that case, that single shift in perspective can activate a chain reaction leading to better exam performance, reduced stress, and a more rewarding professional career. After all, the real magic of motivational talks isn't in the talk itself—it's in the *action* the audience takes afterwards.

I drove away from the campus under the golden hues of the late afternoon sun, feeling a sense of fulfilment. The stories had done their job; the students had done their part by listening, reflecting, and opening up. I found myself silently thanking the lazy poet for teaching us such a lasting lesson: we can have the key in our hands, but if we don't use it before sunset, we might miss out on a treasure we can never retrieve.

That is the power of time management. That is the power of taking action *now* instead of later.

And ultimately, that is the simple, human truth that a story, lovingly told, can convey more deeply than any lecture or instruction manual ever could.

We are all a work in progress; every story starts with a rough draft.
Mine happens to be written in real life.

Part 4:

To Mend, To Make

Books are windows, wide and vast,

To learn from the present and understand the past.

Listening, Learning, and Leading

To Discover Purpose, and to Empower Others

I sometimes look back and laugh at how unaware I was of the path I was about to take. In the early days of my writing career, I stepped into a team leader role for a content creation group. Back then, I barely knew the term "life coaching." All I knew was that I liked helping people. My job might have been to guide their writing, but I found myself doing more than just editing content. I was giving advice, listening to their issues, and suggesting ways to stay motivated. Showing them how to tap into their creativity and self-confidence felt natural.

But this was just a small hint of something bigger. Working with people so closely made me realise that my real spark was helping them see their own potential. Over time, I realised that "leading" a team goes far beyond assigning tasks or setting deadlines. It's about giving people the tools and the environment they need to grow, both in their professional and personal lives. In those early team meetings and late-night editing sessions, I discovered that my true passion involved guiding others to figure out their strengths and face their fears.

Discovering a Passion for Mentorship

Once I recognised how much I enjoyed guiding others, I learned more about mentoring. I wanted to understand what made some people thrive under a mentor's watch while others felt restricted or misunderstood. My search for clarity led me to explore personality development, life coaching methods, parenting approaches, stress management strategies—you name it. I realised I was hungry for knowledge that would help me connect with people more deeply.

One of the biggest lessons I learned was that mentorship isn't just about listing out rules or handing someone a roadmap to success. It's more like standing beside them, shining a flashlight on different paths, and letting them decide which one feels right. Books, online workshops, and specialised courses became my personal arsenal. They offered me frameworks for emotional well-being, communication skills, and motivation techniques. Yet, through all this reading and training, I remembered that real learning doesn't begin or end with a certificate. It grows from applying what you learn to actual life situations. A diploma can look great on the wall, but it's useless if it just stays there gathering dust. What truly matters is how you take that knowledge and weave it into daily interactions—whether you're coaching a colleague through anxiety or helping a friend plan their next big step.

Education as a Personal Journey

I've always believed that genuine education is about transformation. And transformation happens inside each of us—it's not something someone can force on you. A teacher or mentor can say all the right things, give you incredible insights, and still make no impact if you aren't open to receiving them. It's like planting seeds in dry ground. You might have the best seeds in the world, but if the soil isn't ready, those seeds won't bloom.

That's why whenever I learned a new technique or strategy, I tried it out in my own life first. If it didn't resonate with me, if I couldn't see it working in my own daily routine, I wouldn't advise it to my team or clients. The last thing I wanted was to give people empty advice that I didn't even believe in. This approach kept me honest. It also made me more aware of the power of authenticity. When I shared my own stories—my struggles with time management or my own self-doubt—people related to me more deeply; they realised I wasn't just preaching from a textbook. I was living proof that these methods can bring real change.

Birth: The Start of Everything

When you think about the question, "Where does it all begin?" it's easy to trace it back to our earliest moments—birth. Our first teachers are the people who raised us. We might not remember everything consciously, but as kids, we absorb everything that happens around us. We notice every tone of voice, every argument, every laugh. We pick up habits and mindsets from our parents, siblings, or whoever else fills our home. Even our extended family or family friends can leave lasting imprints on our personality.

Some kids are lucky enough to grow up in stable, loving environments. Others deal with chaos or neglect. These early experiences shape how we see the world. If you grow up where problems are openly discussed and solutions are found calmly, you might learn to communicate well and stay resilient. But if you grow up with adults who panic, yell, or ignore issues altogether, you might start shutting down or lashing out when things get tough. These patterns often stick with us into adulthood, even if we don't fully realise it.

The Influence of Parents and Role Models

Watching parents and role models in action teaches us more than just behaviours; it also shows us how to handle success, failure, stress, or big changes. If we see our parents approach problems by calmly talking them out, we might learn to do the same. If they bottle up their emotions, we might copy that instead. Our elders basically lay down an unspoken blueprint for how we think life should work.

Later, we start experimenting with our own unique style—how we speak, how we dress, what we believe in. But no matter how much we branch out, some part of us remains tied to those early lessons. Sometimes, we even fight against them, consciously deciding to be the opposite of what we saw growing up. Either way, our childhood shapes how we view ourselves and others.

Peer Pressure and Society's Demands

Then comes the wonderful or not-so-wonderful world of peer

pressure. Suddenly, we're not just looking at our families but also our classmates and friends. We notice who's popular, who's talented, who seems to sail through life easily. It's a natural human reaction to compare ourselves. But sometimes, parents or teachers unintentionally add to that stress by saying things like, "Look at your friend scoring top marks in math. Why can't you do that?" or "Your cousin is so good at sports; how come you're not joining a team?"

While some kids thrive on this comparison, many feel trapped or judged. They might push themselves into activities they don't actually enjoy just to make someone else happy. Over time, they can lose track of what truly interests them. They become adults who pursue careers or lifestyles that don't match their real passions. And beneath the surface, they might harbour a lot of confusion, resentment, or sadness because they never felt free to explore their own potential.

Growing Up in a Fast-Paced World

As these kids grow into teenagers and young adults, they're greeted by a society that seems to reward speed and instant results. Why spend years perfecting a skill when you can find a shortcut or hack? Why wait for real, deep connections when

This desire for quick outcomes can become a habit that's really hard to break. In small doses, efficiency is great. But when we become obsessed with shortcuts, we miss the value of slow, steady growth. We lose sight of how important it is to build a solid foundation for any skill or relationship. If we keep looking for the fastest way to success, we might end up feeling hollow because deep fulfilment usually comes from putting in the time and effort.

The Allure of Shortcuts

I see it happening all around me. If there's a way to cut corners —whether it's cheating on a test, lying on a resume, or using unethical strategies at work—some people jump at it. Peer pressure can make this problem worse. Maybe someone's friend is already making big money or showing off a glamorous lifestyle online. If we buy into the idea that we're falling behind, we can grow desperate and try anything to catch up.

But shortcuts come with a hidden cost. When we skip essential steps in growth or learning, we remain fragile. The first real challenge or setback can knock us down because we haven't built the resilience that comes from honest effort. And if we repeatedly chase quick rewards, we can become addicted to that dopamine rush without ever stopping to see if we're actually happy or at peace. In the end, we might not even know what genuine satisfaction feels like.

While some kids thrive on this comparison, many feel trapped or judged. They might push themselves into activities they don't actually enjoy just to make someone else happy. Over time, they can lose track of what truly interests them. They become adults who pursue careers or lifestyles that don't match their real passions. And beneath the surface, they might harbour a lot of confusion, resentment, or sadness because they never felt free to explore their own potential.

Obesity of the Mind: Too Much Reward

In a more lighthearted moment, I once described excessive validation-seeking as a kind of "mental obesity." Just like overeating can harm our bodies, constantly chasing "likes," compliments or attention can hurt our emotional well-being. Our brains get used to these dopamine hits, and soon, we need more and more. It becomes an unhealthy cycle where we rely on external praise for our self-worth. Any negative comment or lack of feedback can send us spiralling into doubt or anxiety.

The real problem is that many people don't even notice they're trapped in this cycle until something forces them to face it—like a mental health crisis, a relationship issue, or a major disappointment. At that point, they might really need help. And that's often where therapy or coaching comes in. Some folks might consider it trendy or superficial to "go to therapy" or "hire a life coach," but in reality, it's just a reflection of how many people are starved for non-judgmental support and genuine connection.

Living in the Age of Validation

If you think about it, it's not surprising that people feel lost. We live in a time when everything moves at lightning speed. Social media encourages us to broadcast every moment—whether it's a vacation, a meal, or a random thought—and then watch as people comment or ignore our posts. That instant feedback loop teaches us to seek approval. If we don't get enough likes, we feel like we've failed.

We also see polished versions of everyone else's lives and compare them to our unpolished reality. This can make us feel like our own lives are incomplete or boring, leading us to overcompensate or pursue a lifestyle that isn't true to who we are. As a result, we might invest more energy in portraying a perfect life online than in actually living a meaningful life offline.

Therapy, Judgment, and Venting Out

Because people aren't sure where else to go, therapy or life coaching sessions become these "venting out" spaces. When someone feels they have no one else who will just listen without judging, they turn to a professional. A lot of people who approached me for work issues eventually started sharing personal problems. Sometimes, they just needed to tell their story out loud to organise the chaos in their minds. That's when I realised I was more than just a "team leader" or "mentor." I became a sounding board, a safe place to land their thoughts.

Initially, I felt overwhelmed. I had studied language and had a bit of background in psychology, but I was not fully prepared for the depth of issues people bring to me. So, I went back to learning. I read up on coping strategies, emotional support techniques, and stress management. I kept upgrading my skills, aiming to offer the right kind of help. Eventually, those one-on-one talks became less of a sideline and more of a calling for me.

Stepping into Life Coaching

That's how my official journey in life coaching really started. It was a gradual shift. The same colleagues who needed a listening ear told their friends and family about me. The next thing I knew, people I had never met were reaching out, asking if they could talk. They weren't looking for me to wave a magic wand. They just wanted clarity, someone to help them define their problems and sort out the best way forward.

When someone is tangled up in their own stress, it's astonishing how much clarity they can get just by talking it through. Half of the problem seems to dissolve once they can articulate what's bothering them. The other half is figuring out what action to take. But most people, in my experience, already have some idea of what needs to be done. Their main blockage is fear—especially the fear of failing or making the situation worse.

A Lifelong Learning Process

As a coach, I don't hand out instant solutions. I'd rather guide people to come up with their own. That might seem slower, but it ensures the changes they make are rooted in genuine understanding. When individuals develop their own problem-solving skills, they become more confident in dealing with future challenges. This process taught me that every conversation is also a learning moment for me. Each client has a unique background, a distinct way of talking about their problems, and a different kind of resilience.

I might apply a technique I learned from a course, only to discover it doesn't quite fit this particular person. That forces me to adapt, to think on my feet. Over the years, I've collected a bunch of methods—reframing, presupposition, dissociation, belief change, and future-pacing—but the real key is customising them to each person's needs. People aren't one-size-fits-all. They each have a story that calls for its own blend of approaches.

Defining Problems: The First Step

One of the core pillars of my coaching style is helping people define their problems clearly. Sometimes, they start by saying, "I'm just stressed," or "I feel so lost." That's pretty vague, and it's hard to find a solution if you don't know exactly what the problem is. So, we dig deeper. Is the stress about work deadlines, relationships, personal fears, or maybe financial worries? Once we pinpoint the root, the problem instantly feels a bit more manageable. It's like shining a flashlight on a dark corner. Even if the corner is messy, at least you can see what's there.

When people see their problems in a more concrete form, they often have a surge of relief. They realised, maybe this isn't as gigantic as I've been imagining." Part of why people get stuck is that they keep these issues swirling around in their heads, unstructured. Talking things through in a safe space can break that cycle of confusion and self-doubt.

When Fear Holds Us Back

Most times, it's not that people lack ideas. It's that they're too afraid to test those ideas. They fear the outcome if things don't go as planned, and this can paralyse them into delaying decisions or avoiding them entirely. This ends up creating more stress and a feeling of hopelessness. A huge part of my job is to help people face the possibility of failure so they're not as terrified by it. Once you imagine the worst-case scenario and accept that, anything better than the worst suddenly feels like an accomplishment.

It might seem odd, but preparing for potential failure can actually build confidence. It teaches us that we'll survive the disappointment, and it might even lead us to a better path. This mental shift makes people more willing to take bold yet calculated steps. When fear of failure isn't hanging over them like a dark cloud, they can finally see all the exciting possibilities they'd been ignoring.

Using Reframing and Belief Shifts

I've found reframing to be a powerful tool. Let's say someone is convinced they're doomed after losing a job. We can turn that around: "This could be your chance to explore a field you've always been curious about." It doesn't solve everything in an instant, but it lets them see another perspective. Combined with belief shifting—where we tackle limiting thoughts like "I'm too old" or "I'm not good enough"—we give the mind a chance to breathe and consider fresh options.

Dissociation also helps some people step back from their intense emotions and observe the situation more calmly. It's like watching a scene from a slight distance. You're not ignoring your feelings, but you're not drowning in them, either. This can be especially useful for people who feel overwhelmed by anxiety or heartbreak.

Accepting the Worst and Embracing the Journey

One concept I frequently emphasise is readiness for extreme outcomes. If you can handle the idea of everything going wrong, you lessen the weight of fear. That doesn't mean you expect to fail or you become pessimistic. You're just mentally prepared. And when real life turns out less harsh than your worst-case scenario, you appreciate the outcome more. It also makes you more resilient. Setbacks become lessons instead of signals to give up.

This approach can feel counterintuitive, especially in a culture that loves to say, "Always think positive!" But in my experience, it's better to acknowledge that things might not go our way. It's more grounded in reality. A healthy dose of realism, combined with a hopeful attitude, creates a balanced mindset where you can dream big but still have your feet on the ground.

Emotional Support and Accountability

Along with guiding people to find solutions, I also focus on emotional support. Sometimes, you just need someone to say, "It's going to be okay," or "I understand why this hurts." Validation of feelings can be a huge relief. But I don't stop there. I also encourage accountability. After all, what good is a plan if it stays on paper? I check in with clients about whether they're following through on the steps they set for themselves. If they slip, we explore why and find ways to get back on track.

This balance between empathy and a little push can be tough to manage. You don't want to be so tough that they shut down, but you also don't want to be so lenient that they never grow. So, I try to stay open to their reactions. Some people respond well to firm encouragement; others need gentler nudges. The best way to know is by listening deeply to their concerns and sense of pacing.

Working with Change-Fallacy Ideas

Another obstacle I often see is what I call "change-fallacy" thinking: the belief that change just isn't possible. People say, "This is who I've always been" or "I'm too far gone to learn something new." These statements can feel very real to them.

They can also be a protective mechanism—if you believe you can't change, then you don't have to face the risk of trying.

But I've seen enough transformations to know these beliefs rarely hold water. We're all capable of shifting our habits, thoughts, and outlook, no matter our age or background. The process can be slow and uncomfortable, but it's absolutely achievable with persistence and the right guidance. The main hurdle is persuading someone to let go of the assumption that they're stuck. Once they open up to the possibility of growth, a whole new world appears before them.

Future-Pacing and Visualization

To help people truly embrace that new world, I often use future-pacing and visualisation. It's about imagining yourself living the life you want in realistic detail. For instance, if you want a more fulfilling career, close your eyes and picture a day in your dream job. Imagine what tasks you're doing, how your environment feels, and how you interact with colleagues or clients. The more vivid the image, the more your mind starts believing it can be real.

But it's not just daydreaming. We also map out possible roadblocks. Maybe you'll need extra training, or you'll have to network with the right people. We talk about how to handle setbacks so they don't catch you off guard. This makes the vision feel more concrete. It's the difference between a wish and a strategic plan.

My Ongoing Growth as a Coach

The beauty of coaching is that it's never one-sided. Sure, the client is the focus, but I'm learning and evolving right alongside them. Every person who comes in with a unique perspective or challenge expands my own understanding. Sometimes, I'll think a certain approach should work perfectly, only to realise it doesn't resonate with them at all. That forces me to adapt, pivot, and keep an open mind about other techniques.

This continuous learning keeps me from getting complacent. It also reminds me that I'm not an all-knowing expert who's above everyone else. I'm a human with my own flaws and experiences, using the knowledge and empathy I've gathered to support others. That humility goes a long way in building trust. People can sense when a coach is being genuine as opposed to rattling off generic advice.

Developing My Own Style

Over time, all these experiences crystallised my own coaching style, which is a blend of patience, accountability, empathy, and straightforward communication. My main goal is to help people clarify what they truly want and then hold their hand as they outline the steps to get there. We break big goals into small tasks so they don't feel overwhelming. We set regular check-ins to keep the momentum going.

In this style, I don't shy away from tough conversations, either. If someone is sabotaging their progress or clinging to unhelpful beliefs, I'll call it out—gently but honestly. Growth often involves facing the uncomfortable truths we'd rather ignore. Yet I balance that honesty with compassion because I know change can stir up a lot of insecurities.

The Joy of Seeing Others Succeed

One of the best parts of this journey is watching people transform. Sometimes, they'll tell me about a breakthrough: a new job, a repaired relationship, or just feeling more at peace. It's a privilege to witness these turning points. It reassures me that all the effort—my own continuous learning, the emotional energy I invest in each session, and the client's willingness to do the work—is worth it.

Yet, I don't take sole credit. Their success is ultimately their own. They're the ones who had to push through doubt, fear, and setbacks. I just held up a mirror so they could see themselves more clearly. That's the real magic of coaching. It's about partnership, not a one-way transfer of wisdom.

Life Coaching as a Collaboration

If there's one thing I emphasise again and again, it's that coaching works best as a collaborative effort. I don't see myself as a guru handing down universal truths. Each client has deep knowledge about themselves that I could never fully capture. My role is to ask the right questions, share relevant insights, and hold a supportive space. When we both commit to that process, real breakthroughs happen.

That's also why I encourage clients to be honest and open, even if it feels uncomfortable. If they're holding back, we can't get to the root cause of whatever issue they're facing.

Once the trust is established, they're more likely to explore buried emotions or conflicting desires they didn't even know they had. That's when the real work—and the real progress—begins.

Patience, Persistence, and Celebrations

Change doesn't happen overnight. I've had clients make swift progress for a few weeks, then slip back into old patterns. Instead of scolding them, I remind them that this is part of the journey. Growth often moves in waves—two steps forward, one step back. Over time, the upward trend becomes clear. But it requires patience and persistence from both sides.

That's why I love celebrating small wins. Maybe someone stood up for themselves in a meeting or finally took a weekend off to recharge. These may seem like minor moments, but they represent real mindset shifts. Acknowledging these steps creates momentum. It gives people a boost of confidence to keep going, reminding them that every bit of progress matters.

A Continuous Learning Adventure

I never planned to become a life coach. It evolved naturally from my desire to support people beyond just their writing tasks. Today, as I look at how far I've come, I'm thankful for every late-night research session, every workshop I enrolled in, and every tearful conversation in which a client felt safe to share their deepest fears. Each moment has shaped me into the coach—and person—I am now. And the journey is far from over.

As technology changes and society's pressures evolve, new challenges will arise. I'll need to keep updating my knowledge, learning new techniques, and listening to the experiences of others. That's the adventurous aspect of this job: no two clients are the same, and no single method works for everyone. The excitement lies in figuring out how to adapt and innovate.

So...

Life coaching, for me, isn't just a job or even a career—it's a continuous lesson in empathy, resilience, and the art of transformation. Each person who walks through my door (or logs into a Zoom session) carries their own tapestry of dreams, doubts, and hidden strengths. My role is to help them unravel that tapestry, see its intricate patterns, and decide how to weave it in a way that aligns with who they really are.

I believe that if more people learned basic life skills—like clear communication, emotional regulation, and stress management—starting from childhood, we'd see fewer crises in adulthood. We'd have more fulfilled individuals who understand how to manage both triumphs and failures with grace. We'd have parents teaching their kids how to cope with disappointment or workplaces, prioritising their health and human connection. Until we reach that ideal, I plan to keep doing what I do: offer a space for people to speak, reflect, and redefine themselves at their own pace. The sheer variety of human stories and experiences keeps me humble. It also keeps me fired up because, with every new client, I see firsthand how powerful it can be for someone to finally realise they're not stuck—they can change.

That's the legacy I want to be part of. It's not about big trophies or public accolades but about the quiet moments in which someone recognises their own courage and capacity to grow. By guiding them through that realisation, I also grow—and that, to me, is the ultimate gift of being a life coach. It's a role that pushes me to be more open, more patient, and more attuned to the fact that learning truly never ends. And honestly, I wouldn't have it any other way.

Each book you read, a mind refined,
Unlock the doors and expand your mind.

With every story, a path unfurls,
Reading connects us to infinite worlds.

Notes from the Author

It's true that I juggle between different roles, but each one is a mindful and purposeful engagement for me. Over time, I've noticed that I'm evolving into a better version of myself with a clearer sense of purpose. As I grow, I find my horizons expanding, both in-depth and in reach.

Through it all, one thing has remained constant: my connection to language. No matter what role I play—storyteller, motivational speaker, copy editor, or life coach—language is at the heart of everything I do. Finding the right words, understanding the right context, and staying true to the right purpose have always been my guiding principles. I've seen firsthand how the power of words can work like magic, shaping thoughts, inspiring actions, and creating lasting change.

I often think of language as water and its adaptability to the nature of the land it flows through. If it meets a mountain range, it becomes a spring. If it reaches a coastal land, it forms the sea. When it flows through agricultural fields, it turns into a nurturing river. This analogy beautifully reflects how language moulds itself to fit every situation, just as I adapt my roles to meet the needs of those I work with.

This fluidity of words has been my biggest strength. It helps me connect with people, share stories that inspire them, offer guidance when needed, and edit or refine their thoughts when clarity is required. Words can heal, motivate, and transform, and I've been fortunate to witness their impact in every area of my work.

Every role I take up is not just a task for me; it's an opportunity to grow, learn, and connect with others in a meaningful way. Whether it's crafting stories, motivating someone to take the next step, helping them organise their thoughts, or guiding them through a life challenge, my focus has always been on using language as a tool for positive change.

In many ways, I feel my journey is like water—it flows, adapts, and transforms while staying true to its essence. And that keeps me going—helping others while growing into a better version of myself with every step.

I hope this book finds you well and helps you in your journey as you walked with me through mine, Your story isn't over, so let's grow and make ourselves a good ending.

Warm Regards,

-Judith Woodrow

Glossary

A

- Anchor: A way to link a specific feeling or state to something—a word, a gesture, or even a memory. For example, in storytelling, you can use a certain phrase to create excitement or nostalgia in your audience.
- Association: Connecting thoughts, feelings, or events in a meaningful way. In life coaching, it helps clients tie positive emotions to their goals and make progress.
- Audience Engagement: Techniques to hold the listener's attention, such as asking questions or using relatable anecdotes.
- Authenticity: Being genuine and relatable to create trust and connection with the audience.
- Active Listening: Paying attention to audience feedback, both verbal and non-verbal, to adapt your delivery.

B

- **Belief Systems**: These are the internal rules we live by. They shape our choices and actions. In coaching or homeschooling, helping someone see and change limiting beliefs can unlock their potential.
- **Body Language**: Non-verbal cues that enhance communication and make messages more impactful.
- **Building Rapport**: Creating a bond of trust and understanding. In storytelling or speaking, this helps you connect deeply with your audience.

C

- **Calibration**: Paying close attention to body language, tone, and facial expressions to understand how someone feels. This skill is important in coaching and teaching to better respond to others.
- **Call to Action**: A clear invitation for the audience to take specific steps toward change
- **Chunking**: Breaking down information into smaller, easier parts or grouping it together to see the bigger picture. This helps when simplifying complex ideas in homeschooling, writing, or editing.
- **Character Development**: Building relatable and dynamic characters to engage the audience.
- Conflict and Resolution: Creating tension and providing a satisfying conclusion to captivate listeners.
- **Clarity**: Delivering messages in a way that is easy to understand and follow.
- **Confidence**: Projecting self-assurance to gain trust and inspire belief in your message.

D

- **Dissociation**: Stepping back from a situation to see it from a neutral perspective. This is helpful in storytelling when narrating tough experiences without overwhelming emotions.
- **Dynamic Language Patterns**: Using powerful and engaging words to hold attention. This is especially useful in speaking, writing, and copyediting to make

your message clear and impactful.

- **Delegation**: Assigning tasks to others to lighten your workload and achieve goals faster.

E

- **Embedded Commands**: Subtle suggestions hidden in a sentence that encourages action. For example, in speaking or writing, you might say, "You'll find it easy to explore your creativity here."
- **Emotional State**: The mood or feelings a person is experiencing. Managing this well can create a positive environment, whether you're homeschooling kids or motivating a group.
- **Empathy**: Understanding and relating to your audience's emotions and experiences.

F

- **Framing**: Setting the tone or perspective for how someone sees a story or idea. In storytelling or coaching, framing can influence how people interpret your message.
- **Future Pacing**: Encouraging someone to imagine a positive outcome or result. This is a powerful technique in coaching or speaking to inspire action and confidence.

G

- **Goal Setting**: Defining clear and achievable objectives. It's a core part of coaching and homeschooling, helping people stay focused and motivated.

- **Gestalt Thinking**: Seeing the big picture rather than focusing only on the details. In storytelling, it ensures your story flows smoothly and makes sense.

H

- **Hypnotic Language**: Words and phrases that engage the subconscious mind. In storytelling or speaking, this kind of language can draw people in deeply and keep them captivated.

I

- **Internal Dialogue**: The thoughts we tell ourselves. In coaching, recognising and shifting negative self-talk into positive affirmations can build confidence.
- **Intentionality**: Being purposeful in your actions and words. In writing, editing, or teaching, this ensures clarity and focus.
- **Imagery**: Using descriptive language to paint vivid pictures in the audience's mind.

K

- **Kinesthetic Learning**: Learning by doing or using physical activities. This works well in homeschooling, especially for kids who need hands-on experiences to grasp concepts.

L

- **Language Patterns**: How words are structured to influence people's thoughts. In speaking and writing, using the right language patterns can make your message more compelling.

- **Limiting Beliefs**: Beliefs that hold people back. These need to be identified and overcome in coaching or speaking to help someone grow and succeed.

M

- **Metaphor**: A way to explain an idea by comparing it to something familiar. Metaphors are great for simplifying complex topics in storytelling or writing.
- **Modelling**: Learning by observing and imitating successful behaviours. Homeschooling or coaching helps students or clients adopt effective habits.
- **Mindfulness**: Staying present and aware to make intentional decisions about how time is spent.
- Moral: The lesson or takeaway that gives a story purpose and meaning.

N

- **Neuro-Linguistic Programming (NLP)**: A method that explores how language, thoughts, and behaviours influence results. It's about using this knowledge to communicate effectively and achieve goals.
- **Nominalisations**: Fancy words made from verbs or adjectives that can make writing unclear. In editing, simplifying these words can make sentences stronger and easier to read.

O

- **Outcome Orientation**: Focusing on what you want to

- achieve rather than dwelling on problems. This approach is key in coaching and homeschooling to keep progress on track.

P

- **Pacing**: Matching someone's tone, body language, or pace to build a connection. This works well in coaching, storytelling, and even parenting.
- **Persuasion**: Using logic, emotion, and credibility to influence and inspire others.
- **Pomodoro Technique**: A time management method using intervals of focused work followed by short breaks.
- **Presuppositions**: Assumptions hidden in statements that shape how people think. Positive presuppositions in speaking or writing can inspire change and hope.
- **Prioritisation**: Identifying and focusing on the most important tasks to efficiently use time.
- **Procrastination**: Delaying tasks unnecessarily, often leading to stress and inefficiency.

R

- **Reframing**: Looking at a situation from a different angle to find something positive. This is a powerful technique in coaching and storytelling to shift mindsets.
- **Rapport**: A feeling of trust and connection with others. It's essential in any kind of interaction, whether you're teaching, speaking, or coaching.

S

- **Sensory Acuity: Noticing small details in someone's**
- **Sensory acuity:** Noticing small details in someone's tone, expression, or posture to understand their feelings. This helps in coaching and teaching to address unspoken concerns.
- **Story Arc**: The structure of a story, including the beginning, middle, and end. Understanding this helps make your storytelling clear and engaging.
- **SMART Goals**: Specific, Measurable, Achievable, Relevant, and Time-bound objectives that guide effective planning.
- Storytelling: Incorporating narratives to make speeches memorable and relatable.

T

- **Timeline Therapy**: A technique to help people revisit past events or imagine future outcomes to release emotional blocks or plan better.
- **Tonality**: The emotion and pitch in your voice. This can make your storytelling or speaking more expressive and impactful.
- **Time Blocking**: Allocating specific blocks of time to particular tasks for better focus and productivity.
- Tone: The emotional feel of a story, shaped by word choice and delivery style.

U

- **Unconscious Competence:** When a skill becomes second nature. In homeschooling or coaching, this is the level you aim to reach with practice and learning.
- **Utilisation**: Making the best of whatever resources or situation you have. A key principle in coaching, teaching, and even storytelling.
- **Urgent vs. Important Matrix**: A framework to categorize tasks and focus on what truly matters.

V

- **Visual Language**: Words that paint pictures in the mind. In storytelling and writing, this makes your message vivid and easy to remember.
- **Vision Casting**: Painting a vivid picture of a desired future to motivate and energize the audience.
- **Values Alignment**: Ensuring that actions and goals reflect personal or shared values. In coaching or homeschooling, this helps create a sense of purpose and direction.

W

- **Well-Formed Outcomes**: Clear and specific goals with actionable steps. This principle keeps things focused and achievable in coaching and teaching.

Z

- **Zooming In/Out**: Focusing on details (zooming in) or stepping back to see the whole picture (zooming out). This helps in writing and editing to balance clarity and perspective.

References

- *Bandler, R., & Grinder, J. (1979).* ***Frogs Into Princes: Neuro Linguistic Programming****. Real People Press.*
- *Bandler, R., & Grinder, J. (1982).* ***Reframing: Neuro-Linguistic Programming and the Transformation of Meaning.*** *Real People Press.*
- *Barrett, L. (2020).* ***Listen: How to Find the Words for Tender Conversations.*** *Princeton University Press.*
- *Boeree, G. C. (2001).* ***Theory and Practice of NLP Coaching.*** *Crown House Publishing.*
- *Brown, B. (2010).* ***The Gifts of Imperfection: Let Go of Who You Think You're Supposed to Be and Embrace Who You Are.*** *Hazelden Publishing.*
- *Chomsky, N. (2002).* ***On Nature and Language.*** *Cambridge University Press.*
- *Crystal, D. (2006).* ***The Language Instinct: How the Mind Creates Language.*** *Harper Perennial Modern Classics.*
- *Diamond, J. (1999).* ***Why Zebras Don't Get Ulcers: The Acclaimed Guide to Stress, Stress-Related Diseases, and Coping.*** *Henry Holt and Co.*
- *Doidge, N. (2015).* ***Staying Okay: Mental Health Strategies for the Modern Era.*** *Ballantine Books.*
- *Duckworth, A. (2016).* ***Grit: The Power of Passion and Perseverance.*** *Scribner.*
- *Harris, T. A. (1967).* ***I'm OK – You're OK****. Harper & Row.*
- *Jung, C. G. (1957). The Undiscovered Self Little, Brown (APA 7th Edition)*
- *Jung, C. G. (1956). Symbols of transformation (R. F. C. Hull, Trans.). Princeton University Press.*

- *Miller, D., & Hansen, J. (2021). Chicken Soup for the Soul: The Advice That Changed My Life. Chicken Soup for the Soul*
- *Kahneman, D. (2011).* ***Thinking, Fast and Slow.*** *Farrar, Straus and Giroux.*
- *Miller, D., & Hansen, J. (2013).* ***Chicken Soup for the Soul: Inspiration for Writers.*** *Chicken Soup for the Soul.*
- *Pinker, S. (2007).* ***The Stuff of Thought: Language as a Window into Human Nature.*** *Viking.*
- *Pressfield, S. (2002).* ***The War of Art: Break Through the Blocks and Win Your Inner Creative Battles.*** *Black Irish Entertainment.*
- *Robertson, D. (2020).* ***Atomic Habits: Tiny Changes, Remarkable Results.*** *Avery.*
- *Roediger, H. L., & Karpicke, J. D. (2006).* ***The Science of Storytelling: How Stories Make Us Human****. Canongate Books.*
- *Seligman, M. E. P. (2018).* ***Reframing Reality: NLP in Real Life****. Crown House Publishing.*
- *Seligman, M. E. P., & Evans, M. J. (1999).* ***Words That Change Minds: Mastering the Language of Influence****. Crown House Publishing.*
- *Sennett, R. (2005).* ***Metamorphosis****. Pantheon Books.*
- *Smith, A. (2017).* ***Endangered Minds: Why Children Don't Think and What We Can Do About It****. Touchstone.*
- *Suess, Dr. (1960).* ***Dr. Seuss Collection****. Random House.*
- *Tannen, D. (1984).* ***Winnie the Pooh Collection****. Penguin Random House.*

- *Teller, D. (1997).* ***Aesop's Fables for Children***. *Dover Publications.*
- *Vonnegut, K. (1989).* ***Nine Stories***. *Random House.*
- *Walton, S. (2005).* ***Disney's Magic English***. *Grolier.*
- *Zimbardo, P. (2007).* ***The Lucifer Effect: Understanding How Good People Turn Evil***. *Random House.*

Judith Woodrow's Poetry Collection:

Echoes of the Heart and Soul

Black & White Edition

JUDITH WOODROW

EDITED BY MS PEANUT WOODROW

Ms Peanut's (Judith's Daughter's) books:

For older readers:

June Woodrow's (Judith's Younger Daughter's) books:

Book 1

Book 2

www.ingramcontent.com/pod-product-compliance
Lightning Source LLC
LaVergne TN
LVHW091305150826
845673LV00006B/1545

* 9 7 9 8 8 9 6 9 9 7 2 5 2 *